DEVOTIONAL COMPANION

TO THE INTERNATIONAL
LESSONS 2000–2001

Usable with All Popular Lesson Annuals

JEFFREY A. RASCHE

ABINGDON PRESS
Nashville

DEVOTIONAL COMPANION TO THE INTERNATIONAL LESSONS 2000–2001

Copyright © 2000 by Abingdon Press

This book is printed on recycled, acid-free, elemental-chlorine–free paper.

ISSN 1074-9918
ISBN 0-687-08724-4

Scripture quotations, unless otherwise indicated, are from the New Revised Standard Version of the Bible. Copyright © 1989 by the Division of Christian Education of the National Council of the Churches of Christ in the United States of America. Used by permission.

Scripture quotations noted TEV are from Today's English Version—Old Testament: Copyright © American Bible Society 1976; New Testament: Copyright © American Bible Society 1966, 1971, 1976, 1992. Used by permission.

The Optimist International creed on page 80 is used by permission of Optimist International, St. Louis, Missouri.

00 01 02 03 04 05 06 07 08 09 — 10 9 8 7 6 5 4 3 2 1

MANUFACTURED IN THE UNITED STATES OF AMERICA

Hymnals Referenced

B Forbis, Wesley, ed. *The Baptist Hymnal*. Nashville: Convention Press, 1991.

C *The Cokesbury Worship Hymnal*. Nashville: Abingdon Press, 1966.

E Glover, Raymond, ed. *The Hymnal 1982*. New York: The Church Hymnal Corporation, 1985.

F Bock, Fred, ed. *Hymns for the Family of God*. Nashville: Paragon Associates, Inc., 1976.

L *Lutheran Book of Worship*. Minneapolis: Augsburg Publishing House, 1978.

P McKim, LindaJo, ed. *The Presbyterian Hymnal*. Louisville: Westminster/John Knox Press, 1990.

UM Young, Carlton R., ed. *The United Methodist Hymnal*. Nashville: The United Methodist Publishing House, 1989.

W Batastini, Robert J., ed. *Worship*. Chicago: GIA Publications, 1986.

Be an Encourager

Hearing the Word

Imagine what it would be like to have terrible legal troubles or a dread disease. It would be frightening to face alone; and even with the presence of a comforting friend to stand by you, the prospects for the future would still be bleak.

Then enters a star lawyer for your legal troubles, or a doctor well known for curing your disease. Suddenly everything changes! By their power and expertise, they are able to solve your legal troubles, or cure your dread disease. Suddenly you are given a new lease on life.

On a "feelings" level, this is the same story behind Psalm 68, except our powerful advocate is God. The particular problems mentioned are only examples: being an orphan or widow; lonely; or in prison. The psalm also mentions God's "enemies," both the wicked and particular historical armies (such as Pharaoh's).

Living the Word

On a television infomercial, one woman told of a frightening personal experience. While shopping at a department store, she selected an eyebrow pencil to purchase. The eyebrow pencil kept falling between the metal wires of her shopping cart, so she laid the cheap item on top of her purse. She forgot it was there until, walking out of the store, she was arrested for shoplifting. She tried to explain. Unfortunately for her, "I forgot I had put it on my purse" is not an excuse that carries a lot of weight with security guards. Even though she had never committed a crime, she was taken to jail. She needed legal help. The story has a happy ending: She got a good lawyer, who straightened out the whole mess—a mess she was no longer able to control on her own.

5

Many situations in life create for us a mess that we can no longer control. Health problems frequently do that. That may be why many people turn to God while waiting for the results of a lump test, or while praying and pacing helplessly in a hospital waiting room. Why do we pray so fervently at those times, but not pray so often after we see the fall colors or successfully zip up our own coat without help?

Other situations that can suddenly make us realize that we need God are a job loss, financial catastrophe, or the death of a loved one. Some ethical dilemmas in our work give us sleepless nights. Some kinds of physical pain, mental anguish, or relationship problems can seem impossible to tolerate or to solve on our own: a rebellious child on drugs; prolonged grief; a boss who fills the workplace with sexual innuendoes; a spouse whose sarcasm bites like an alligator.

All of these things we can easily identify as our "enemies," for they threaten our peace and well-being. We want and need God to rise up and defeat these enemies, for we are often powerless to overcome them on our own. In this way, the psalm has special meaning for us. "God rises up and scatters his enemies. . . . As smoke is blown away, so he drives them off" (vv. 1-2 TEV). When our problems disappear, we can rejoice, just like the psalmist urges us to do.

Of course, we may wish to question the basic truth of this psalm, particularly when our problems have not vanished. Does God always intervene on our behalf? Does God always scatter our enemies? It would be nice if God would make all of our most stubborn problems disappear like smoke in the wind, but sometimes they just hang around.

In those cases, this psalm at least gives us hope. God is more than a friend to walk beside us, though God certainly is that. This psalm reminds us that God is powerful—like a good lawyer is to a legal case, like an expert doctor is to a medical case. With God, the end of the story has not yet been told until every enemy of our peace and well-being is defeated and we can all join together in the celebration.

Let us pray:
Lord, we pray you would take our problems from us and defeat those things that are enemies to our joy in life. In the meantime help us to wait with hope, that we may see through the smoke of difficulty and pain your Holy Spirit blowing like a wind to revive and refresh us. In the name of Christ, Amen.

SUGGESTED PSALM: *Psalm 112*

SUGGESTED HYMNS:

"*Jesus Calls Us*" *(B, C, E, F, L, UM)*

"*Take My Life, and Let It Be*" *(B, C, E, L, P, UM, W)*

Be Obedient

Hearing the Word

It is natural to wonder about great leaders, How did they become leaders? or By what authority do they lead us? Accordingly, the Bible relates the "call stories" of many of its great leaders. Joshua 1:1-9 records God calling Joshua to succeed Moses and lead the Israelites into the promised land. This call story includes more than mere marching orders; it also contains instructions about attitude (when God called Moses in Exodus 3, it is clear Moses needed to work on his attitude too). Joshua is told to approach the job with determination and confidence. This call following Moses' death is no surprise to Joshua or the people; during Moses' life, God had already indicated that Joshua would succeed Moses (see Deuteronomy 31:14-29, especially verse 23).

Living the Word

The call of Joshua would be fun to preach on for three Sundays in a row, and each sermon could have an entirely different point. One sermon might easily focus on the two-way nature of our relationship with God. God gave the Israelites the land to possess, but in exchange he wanted their obedience. In the same way, we should still thank God for the gifts we receive, and seek to obey God.

Another good sermon could be a reminder that God's story is often told in chapters, in periods of time defined by events instead of the clock. There are different leaders for different times, but over time the story is still God's. Even someone as great as Moses could be replaced when the time came. For the rest of us, we need to keep the faith that God will always be able to find leaders for the church, and not "worship" some past leader. We should adapt to new leaders, and appreciate their unique gifts. The God who called the beloved old church leader is the same God who called the new one.

But I think my favorite sermon would be based on the words found both in Deuteronomy and the call story in Joshua 1:1-9. "Be determined and confident." This phrase appears three times in the nine verses of Joshua 1:1-9, and once in Deuteronomy 31:23. In school, when a teacher repeats something four times, it is a good idea to remember it.

Really, it is a message we all need to hear. Joshua had a fearsome task: He had to lead the people like an army and take over a whole country! It was hazardous work, but God reminded him to remember that the land he would pass over was already given to the Israelites. In other words, God had already given him the victory; Joshua just needed to live it out.

What if we were to approach our lives that same way, with confidence that God is already at work to bring about a joyous and just conclusion? For example, it is easy for us to talk about how much we wish our church could grow, but it is easier to cower in the pew and look out the door at the busy city or country life than it is to approach evangelism with determination and confidence. If we felt assured that God is working with us to help our church grow, it may not be so intimidating to ask a friend to come to church.

Another example: Someone prays once; their prayer does not seem to get answered, so they quit praying. I understand too; it is discouraging. But remember that Jesus taught his disciples to be determined and persistent in prayer. The world is a wilderness, and the problems that face the world are stubborn. It will take determined and confident people to address the problems. The Lord has called us all to do just that. Be determined and confident, for the Lord is with you. Again, be determined and confident; and don't forget, be determined and confident. Yes, even for a fourth time, so that none of us will ever forget it: Be determined! Be confident! For indeed the Lord is with us in our work.

Let us pray:
Lord, adjust our attitudes today. Too often we ooze defeat and pessimism. Forgive us for complaining so much, and for wishing so often without a single plan of action. Instead, Lord, mobilize us and encourage us. Help us to forget our fears and to remember your presence, that we might have our confidence restored and our determination renewed. This we ask through Christ our Lord, Amen.

READ IN YOUR BIBLE: *Psalm 145:14-20*   **September 17, 2000**
SUGGESTED PSALM: *Psalm 104:10-30*
SUGGESTED HYMNS:
  "Let All the World in Every Corner Sing" (B, C, E, P, UM, W)
  "Let Us Break Bread Together" (B, E, F, L, P, UM, W)

Be Faithful

Hearing the Word

Psalm 145 is an acrostic. That is, it is composed of twenty-one lines, each beginning with a letter of the Hebrew alphabet and arranged in alphabetical order. A few other psalms, including 119, follow this general structure. The point of the structure, besides being an interesting literary challenge, is to convey a sense of completeness (that is, God is to be praised in everything, from A to Z). Psalm 145 is popular; it is used four times in the current Revised Common Lectionary as the Sunday Service psalm. It opens the closing section of Psalms, and each of the five psalms that compose the end of the book begin and end with the exclamation "Praise the Lord" or "Hallelujah."

Living the Word

Our household includes one dog, four cats, a salt-water and two freshwater aquariums, and two land hermit crabs. We also had a snake once, but it was uninvited and soon was expelled. The other animals, though, all have one thing in common: They love dinnertime. The dog, a Sheltie, can be in a dead sleep, her paws moving as she dreams of chasing cats all over the yard. But as soon as one of the kids opens her bag of food, she is instantly on her feet, wide-eyed and prancing everywhere like she cannot wait one more second for that bowl of food to be set in front of her. The cats enjoy cat food in their own dignified way; but if our family is eating chicken, they have learned to expect tidbits. You feel a pawing on your thigh, and look down, and there is an orange furry face looking up at you with pleading eyes that say "Oh, please!" over and over again.

9

The fish lead a life of quiet serenity; but as soon as that stinky dry food hits the surface, they revert to their piranha imitation for five wild minutes. They cannot say "thank you," being underwater, but if they could they would. You can tell.

That all comes to mind when I read Psalm 145:15-16: "All living things look hopefully to you, and you give them food when they need it. You give them enough and satisfy the needs of all" (TEV). The psalmist goes on to describe God as merciful and righteous in all God does, and as a supplier of needs who hears the cries of all living creatures.

Reading this psalm, however, turns our next thought to the people in the world who are hungry. There are many causes for hunger; it has no simple answer. Surely it must offend God for us to turn our backs on the hungry while blaming them for overpopulating. The most recent statistics indicate that one person dies as a result of hunger or hunger-related disease at the rate of one person every 2.5 seconds around the clock. That means that during an average twenty-minute sermon, four hundred eighty people will die of hunger. If the sermon is good, it will make the people in the congregation thankful for their many blessings. Perhaps we will become increasingly sensitive to the eyes of the poor, who depend on God for life too. When we see their eyes on TV, they seem to be looking at us, as though they think God might be about ready to work through us! And those eyes are looking for hope, like verse 15 says. So when God moves us to be generous, it is one way God is in us, working to provide a little hope for the hungry.

So yes, let us be thankful, for God has provided for our needs. But second, let us be part of providing for others, for it should be true that God is in us and works through us. Today is a good day to take whatever it is you have previously given toward fighting world hunger, multiply it by ten or even a hundred, and then send that amount twice as often. If you could be that generous, it still may not stop the problem; but remember how happy the animals are to eat, and think about how much more joy such generosity would bring to those who are hungry.

Let us pray:

For our many gifts and blessings, Lord, we truly thank and praise you. For those who lack food, may we be one way that you can bless them. In the name of Christ, who fed the multitude until all had eaten enough. Amen.

"God of Grace and God of Glory" (B, C, E, F, L, P, UM)
"Jesus Shall Reign" (All)

Be an Example

Hearing the Word

One of the recurring themes in Jesus' teaching is to be prepared and watchful and to wait for the coming of the Son of Man. These particular verses are unique to Luke, although the next parable (the faithful and unfaithful servants) can be found in both Luke and Matthew. Typically, today the text is interpreted to mean being ready for the second coming of Christ, or simply being prepared to receive insights and growth from the Lord. But what did Jesus mean by this teaching, since he was already with the disciples? Probably Jesus meant being prepared for a radical new faith, although he could have been referring to a time after his own death. In any case, today's lesson scripture ties into this theme of being ready. Remember, Samuel could receive God's calling only when he was prepared and listening to the right voice. He was ready when he said, "Speak, Lord, for your servant is listening."

Living the Word

Many pastors run a country mile out in front of their congregations. Like a little kid on a hike, they are not always patient with a comfortable pace for change and new ideas. So they suggest plans that may seem like a good idea, and then are surprised that some committee did not leap on their idea and celebrate it like it was the invention of putting butter on bread.

Think of it from the point of view of a particular committee—for example, the education committee. They work all day, or battle small children and laundry and the supper dishes, and get everybody back out the door to their games and meetings. Then they drag themselves to the church, go to the basement, and sit in a folding chair under the fluorescent light, hoping the meeting will last only one hour this time. Then in pops the minister, who got a great idea in the middle of the night last night and has been thinking all day about how wonderful it would be to rent a circus tent for Vacation Bible School this year. He tells the committee that it will only cost $500 for the week, which seems like a small price to pay for all that community visibility in the small town (as if there is anybody in town who didn't already know that church has a Vacation Bible School every second week of August).

So, what do you think the vote will be? Most likely, on that night the minister is going to go home disappointed.

Now, suppose this scene unfolded a bit differently. Suppose that two months before, the people and the pastor decided to study new ways to reach the people in the community who had not so far responded in any way to the church. Suppose that they identified a lot of unchurched children in the neighborhood, plus they suspected many of those parents would not feel comfortable with a traditional church worship experience. Suppose that at the last education committee meeting, someone came up with the idea of having several worship services in other locations around town and at non-Sunday morning times. Finally, suppose that a week or two before this meeting, the minister passed around a brochure from the rental tent company so that everyone could see how much the tents cost and what they look like. This time when the committee meets, they are actively searching for new ideas instead of merely hoping to get out of there in an hour.

In the same way, to follow Christ means to be ready for change, for new direction, for new ideas, and thus, for newness of life. How do we make ourselves ready? We can pray a lot, read the Bible, and go to church regularly. We can train ourselves to listen for God's leading, and realize that the Lord is going to change our life. Our values, daily schedule, habits, words and thoughts, emotions, relationships, and our eternal destiny will change. But first we must be ready, at any time, at all times. Be ready for the coming of the Lord!

Let us pray:

Lord, we know you speak to us all the time, but so often your words are drowned out by the background noise in our life. Teach us to make our life the kind of setting in which you can speak and be heard, and your work can easily be done, both on us spiritually and through us on the world. Through Christ, our Lord. Amen.

READ IN YOUR BIBLE: *Psalm 119:1-8*   October 1, 2000

SUGGESTED PSALM: *Psalm 1*

SUGGESTED HYMNS:

"*Lord, I Want to Be a Christian*" *(B, C, F, P, UM)*

"*Holy God, We Praise Thy Name*" *(E, F, L, P, UM, W)*

The Challenge of Change

Hearing the Word

Psalm 119, like Psalm 145 which we considered in September, is an acrostic. However, Psalm 119 takes the form to an extreme. Instead of one line of verse for each letter of the Hebrew alphabet (arranged in alphabetical order), Psalm 119 has eight lines for each letter (in English, it would be like eight lines beginning with *A*, then eight beginning with *B*, and so on). Further, with some exceptions, each line includes one of the following eight words which describe some aspect of the Law (in the New Revised Standard Version, they are translated as "law," "decrees," "statutes," "commandments," "ordinances," "word," "precepts," and "promise"). It is interesting to go through and underline or highlight these words in each verse. This psalm, through its repetition and subtle variation, is valuable for meditation. Compare it with Psalms 1 and 19 for content.

Living the Word

At a church campground, someone put up a homemade sign at the edge of the pond. The message was ambiguous: "Fishing for Campers Only." It is a good rule, especially if a camper falls in. Then again one might assume that if a person accidentally caught a fish, he or she would have to throw it back.

There is another sign on the same pond. It says, "No Fishing for Bass." Apparently someone just has a gift for ambiguity. The sign works too, for no bass have ever gone fishing there.

Actually, it is more difficult to write a rule down than one might think. Some lawyers and accountants make a good living helping people find loopholes in the government's laws and tax rules, and others work to "close the loopholes" so that people cannot get by the intended rule on a technicality.

Society is full of rules. We have rules for board games and an official rule book for each level of baseball. Each state has its rules of the road, and the federal government has thousands of rules that relate to income taxes. Why do we have rules? Where do they come from? And what events lead us to want to create a new rule? How does this help us understand God's rules for us?

Back to the pond: It is a safe guess that "outsiders" who were effective fishermen were coming so often that they threatened to fish all the bass out of the pond. Thus the rules were born. They were intended to help people but, like all rules, they place limits on some in order to accomplish a good thing for others. Outsiders cannot fish there, and anyone who catches a bass has to throw it back. But the rule is good because it means campers should always have a chance to catch a big fish.

We often focus on the limitations rules put on us. Truthfully, there are many times people even want to, and do, break God's laws. As someone once said, "Rules were made to be broken." But that is not the case with God's rules. They were not made to be a burden, but to teach us a better way of life.

Psalm 119 focuses on the benefits, not the limitations, of God's laws. The psalm points out that obeying the Law helps keep us from being put to shame (one only needs to read the newspapers to see many examples of the consequences and public embarrassment people suffer who break God's laws). Psalm 119 points out that obedience to God's laws is one recipe for true happiness (and isn't that true?). The psalm also points out that we can trust the guidance the Law offers us; we will never be misled if we are keeping the Law. The laws of God are given to help us live a better, happier, more fulfilled life. They may limit us, but they limit us from making choices that are harmful to us or others. We are not always grateful for being given a list of rules to follow, but the rules God has given us to follow are indeed a gift.

Let us pray:
Lord, thank you for caring enough for us to give us guidance in the form of your laws and commands. Help us be wise enough to follow your way, and forgive us when we rebel against your laws. In the name of Christ, who forgives, heals, and gives us another chance. Amen.

READ IN YOUR BIBLE: *Isaiah 55:6-11*   **October 8, 2000**

SUGGESTED PSALM: *Psalm 113*

SUGGESTED HYMNS:

"Holy, Holy, Holy" (All)

"Thine Be the Glory" (B, F, L, P, UM)

The Challenge of Choosing

Hearing the Word

The book of Isaiah is often divided into three parts, based on the historical context of each part. First Isaiah consists of chapters 1 through 39, and was written before the Babylonian Empire crushed Judah (and Jerusalem) and sent the survivors out of the promised land and into exile. Second Isaiah consists of chapters 40 through 55. It was written to encourage the exiles that God could still restore them. Third Isaiah, chapters 56 through 66, was written in a troubled time after the process of restoring the promised land had begun. Thus today's devotional text comes at the end of the prophet's words that were intended to comfort the suffering exiles. It is linked to today's lesson scripture by the declaration that God does not see the same way people see.

Living the Word

A clever "Far Side" cartoon by Gary Larson contrasted what people say and what dogs hear. While the owner was carrying on quite a conversation with his pet, all the dog could hear was "blah, blah, blah."

Humans have a tendency to anthropomorphize (which means to convey human characteristics on nonhuman things). When a tree is cut down, there are those who talk like the tree is sad or even in pain. (But remember—it is made of wood. Maybe *we* feel sad about the tree, but it has no brain.) Likewise, we give cars a personality, exclaim that our computer "doesn't like it when I do that," and sometimes we even transfer our feelings onto God. When we impose our thoughts and feelings on nonhuman creatures or things, it can be funny or even comforting, but it is not real.

Interestingly, in Christ's birth, God came to earth to be like us, so that we know that God understands us and has experienced our life firsthand. It would be a little like us volunteering to be a dog for a while. It would certainly help bridge the understanding both ways, and make us feel even closer to the species than we do now. We have the tendency to think of God as just another version of ourselves. God became human and dwelt among us not because God is simply a super-sized human being, but because God is different from us in important ways.

Both the lesson and the devotional scripture today remind us of that. We cannot comprehend God and God's ways anymore than a dog can get past "blah, blah, blah" by listening to us talk. What we know about God has primarily been revealed in the life of Jesus Christ. Jesus' coming was a special gift of communication.

Our faith is stronger and more accurate when it is based on the reality that God is different, not just a larger version of ourselves. Like a creator is categorically different from his/her creation, God is different from us. Yet that difference is good. For example, this scripture points out that God must be much more forgiving than we are. People tend to think there is a point when we have messed up beyond help. But God's mercy goes so far beyond human understanding that it is difficult for us to understand, and certainly to practice. Love and mercy are two things we really need from God.

Just as a human being knows far more than his or her dog or cat, God's thoughts and ways are far above our comprehension. But just as a human being can deeply love a cat or dog (and the feelings seem to be mutual), through Christ, we have been given a glimpse of God's love for us. God is different from us, but that is good.

Let us pray:
We come before you, Lord, as clay pots about to speak to the Potter who made them. Thank you for caring about our thoughts, our joys, and our sorrows. Help our respect for you to grow as we remind ourselves that you are not just another clay vessel like us. Help our faith and confidence in you to grow as we ponder your awesome power, your love, and your mercy. Bless and guide us, Lord, that we may be what you have made us to become. Through Christ our Lord, Amen.

The Challenge of Loss

Hearing the Word

Grief is a part of life that transcends all cultures, times, and places. King David, Israel's greatest king, expresses his grief in today's lesson scripture (see 2 Samuel 1:17-20, 22-27). The devotional scripture for today is Psalm 77:1-9. These verses capture the feeling of loss in a vivid and poetic manner. The selection ends with several deep questions about God's nature and work. Such questions are a natural part of grief. The feeling that God is no longer in control of the events of this world is also a powerful expression of grief. The psalm continues by remembering some of God's past miracles, and gradually, as the passage continues, faith seems to return. Although the process generally takes longer in life, this psalm expresses the pattern of grief, questioning, remembering, and renewed faith.

Living the Word

As this is being written the news is dominated by the school shootings in Littleton, Colorado, on April 20, 1999. Two heavily armed students opened fire on their classmates, killing one teacher, twelve students, and finally themselves. They seriously wounded many more students.

Tragedy and grief often leave us with profound questions. Some of the questions in this case center on school security measures, how to keep such sophisticated firearms and bombs out of the hands of high school students, and the motivation of the perpetrators. Other questions have been like the ones in today's scripture: Why did God let this happen? Did God abandon us or reject us? Has God's anger taken the place of God's compassion? Is God as powerful as we have always thought, and if so, why didn't God make all those bullets miss those precious students and their teacher?

In the book of Job, Job had three friends who tried for forty or so chapters to answer his questions in the midst of his suffering, but it never made him suffer less. Their answers angered Job instead of comforting him. They were much better friends when they kept quiet and sat in the ashes with him; then he at least knew he had someone with him in his suffering. And that is the true source of comfort, insofar as comfort is possible in the midst of grief. After all, doesn't Psalm 23:4 say, "Even though I walk through the darkest valley, I fear no evil; for you are with me"? This refers to the comfort of God's presence, but it could apply to the ministry of the presence of friends, too.

If we want to be true friends, like Job's friends were before they got up from sitting in the ashes with him and opened their mouths, then we will learn to sit in the ashes, with closed mouths, with those people who suffer. Let questions fill the air. There is a time and place for questions. Who are they going to hurt? God? Relax. God is big enough to handle being questioned. God doesn't need us for lawyers, but God does need us to be true friends of those who grieve. That means to give a hug, to hold a hand, to shed a sympathizing tear. It means to say "I'm sorry you are in so much pain," but not try in vain to take the pain away with words or jokes or distractions, and certainly not with lame theological rationalizations.

On the cross, Jesus asked God, "Why have you forsaken me?" It is the basic question of suffering that most of us ask at some time in life. Even for Jesus, no answer boomed down from heaven. That day there was only the echo of his question, and suffering. I do believe that in time what we see dimly, or not at all, will be seen more clearly. In the meantime, what the world needs is fewer people who try to answer the impossible questions of suffering, and more people who will sit in the ashes with those who suffer.

Let us pray:
Dear Lord, help me have enough faith to endure the questions of this life, and wait in peace and confidence for your answers given in your time. Help me to show love and compassion to those who suffer, and to know that in my own difficult times you are with me, like a good friend would be. Amen.

SUGGESTED PSALM: *Psalm 78:1-8*

SUGGESTED HYMNS:

"Savior, Like a Shepherd Lead Us" (B, C, E, F, L, P, UM)
"My Shepherd Will Supply My Need" (B, E, F, P, W)

The Challenge of Leadership

Hearing the Word

At first glance this psalm appears to be a long rehearsal of Jewish history. In wisdom-teaching style, the interpretation of history draws a sharp contrast between God's faithfulness to the people and the people's rebelliousness against God. A modern reader might say, "Ho hum, that is not a new story." But the fact that this psalm ends with David's anointing provides a clue to the psalmist's motivations. The psalm offers an explanation concerning why God abandoned the leaders who came from the northern tribes in favor of David, who came from the south (Judah). The unfaithfulness of the people explains why Jerusalem, in the south, became the location of God's temple and the center of centralized Jewish rule under David. Today's lesson scripture, from 2 Samuel 2 and 5, is closely parallel to Psalm 78 because both deal with David's anointing as king.

Living the Word

David was only thirty years old when he began his reign as king of Israel. Being a king must feel like a heavy responsibility, especially for someone of that age. The Scripture refers to him as a "shepherd." Can you imagine trying to take care of the problems of a whole country, and a brand new one at that? He did not have the benefit of automobiles or modern communication devices to help gather everyone together. So he was "shepherd" of a "flock" so big that it would take him days or weeks just to travel across

Israel, let alone deal with the people's problems and issues. In short, he needed a lot of people to help him shoulder the burden of "shepherding" so many people.

Like King David, pastors are sometimes compared to shepherds. First, they are charged with the responsibility to help the people avoid problems and other pitfalls in life. Most pastors preach and warn their flock about dangers such as drug and alcohol abuse, gambling, domestic violence, and so on. Yet when someone does "fall," as in the case of a crime, addiction, or marital problem, the pastor is usually there to help care for that person.

Second, pastors are given the responsibility of keeping the flock together. That is not always easy. How do you keep two people together in church when they are determined to fight with each other? Sometimes churches are faced with difficult and controversial issues.

Third, there is the responsibility to look out for lost sheep. Have you ever tried to list all the people who are *not* at church on a given Sunday? It is easy to say "Just go talk to them," but how many people can you schedule an appointment with, even if you abandon your family and church meetings and schedule all seven evenings?

All this is not to complain that the job of shepherding is too hard for one person to do. There is a more important message here than evoking sympathy for pastors. The message is that there is an awful lot of shepherding to do in any community. There are a lot of people who are in the hospital feeling depressed, or facing marital troubles. There are plenty of youth who need someone to talk to them and lead them on the right way, and a lot of children who need someone's good example to follow.

What every church needs, and the world needs, are more good shepherds who will watch for the fallen, guide the lost, comfort the hurting, and pick up the helpless. To do this you don't have to be a pastor; shepherding is really the work of all Christians.

Let us pray:
We pray today for the lost and hurting people of our family, our community, and our world. Help them to know that they are always in your sight and in your care. We invite you to do your shepherding work through us, so that we may be instruments of your love and comfort and guidance. May all of your beloved flock become as one, and follow in your footsteps. Amen.

SUGGESTED PSALM: *Psalm 93*
SUGGESTED HYMNS:
  "Hope of the World" (E, L, P, UM, W)
  "Open My Eyes, That I May See" (B, C, F, P, UM)

The Challenge of God's Promise

Hearing the Word

Imagine buying your dream house and, after years of anticipation, finally moving in. Once everything is settled and you are finally ready to begin living in it, there could well be a moment to stop and be thankful. This devotional scripture reading captures a moment much like that. One of the huge accomplishments of King Solomon's career was to build a temple for the Lord. This was no small task; it was an awe-inspiring architectural achievement that took many workers and many years to build. So when God "moved in," symbolized by placing the ark of the covenant (containing the tablets of the Ten Commandments) in its special place, it was a moment to savor and give thanks. The devotional scripture is linked to the lesson text (2 Samuel 7:1-13) because King David had dreamed of building the temple, but it was his son, King Solomon, who finally fulfilled the dream in God's own time.

Living the Word

More than fifteen hundred years before King Solomon had the majestic Temple built in Jerusalem, Pharaoh Khufu (Cheops) of Egypt had some ambitious building plans of his own. The Great Pyramid still stands today, and is considered one of the "Seven Wonders of the World." Without the benefit of modern instruments or equipment, tens of thousands of workers spent twenty years building a structure that covers 13 acres at its base and that stands as tall as a 40-story building! It is staggering simply to consider the work of carving approximately 2.3 million solid limestone blocks that average 5,000 pounds apiece.

Why was the Great Pyramid built? The pharaoh wanted to build a tomb for himself. He forced a multitude of people to serve his self-centered goal of preserving his physical body forever. By contrast, the Temple Solomon built provided a place for hundreds of thousands of Israelites to worship God. It is terribly ironic that the pyramids, built to preserve their royal occupants after death, were routinely ransacked and robbed, making the effort required to build them time spent in vain. Yet, what about the Temple that King Solomon built? Eventually it was destroyed but its central purpose, the glorification and worship of God, continues to this day.

Churches that exist to serve God and other people are alive and well, no matter what happens to the building. On the other hand, churches that exist to protect the structure and serve themselves have already failed. To illustrate this principle, attend a church meeting and make a motion to donate $50 to world hunger. Typically, a self-centered church will not want to give $50 to starving people due to high utilities and other expenses relating to the upkeep of the local church. Perhaps someone will make the standard point about the need to help our own local people before we send money overseas. Thousands of refugees can be starving to death, but in a self-centered church the motion to donate even $50 will likely get defeated, even though most of the people sitting around the table have $50 in their wallets!

It would be better to let the roof fall in and to serve the Lord than to be more passionate about the building than the needy. The Great Pyramid may live on, but the one for whom it was built to serve is dead and his riches are plundered. The Great Temple built in Solomon's day may be long gone, but the God and the community of faith it was built to serve live on.

Let us pray:

Help us be at least as generous and excited about the needs of the helpless as we are about our own leaky roofs and our remodeling projects. Forgive our idolatry of buildings, and remember our mission. In the name of Jesus, whose ministry lives and grows even though he never had a building to call his own. Amen.

READ IN YOUR BIBLE: *Numbers 15:30-31*   **November 5, 2000**

SUGGESTED PSALM: *Psalm 51*

SUGGESTED HYMNS:

"*Just As I Am, Without One Plea*" *(B, C, E, F, P, UM)*

"*Breathe on Me, Breath of God*" *(B, E, F, L, P, UM, W)*

When Believers Fall

Hearing the Word

The two verses of the devotional reading sound as though they spell death for most or all people; after all, who has never sinned intentionally? However, it is important to consider these two verses in the context of the section of Scripture in which they are found (see especially vv. 22-35). The main point deals with the issue of someone who unintentionally breaks the Law. Can that person be forgiven, or is he or she condemned to die? The answer is that there is a means of grace; an animal sacrifice can be offered to atone for the unintentional sins of humans. However, this section, overall, powerfully makes the point that animal sacrifice was not designed as a way for us to sin freely and then kill a lot of animals to transfer our responsibility onto some poor innocent creature. Christians do not base our faith on such a legalistic system, but it is important to see that even then sacrifice offered a possible means of grace.

The following story about a man who was put to death for merely gathering firewood on the Sabbath should perhaps be understood in the category of "making an example" for the sake of teaching, and not as a genuine picture of typical Jewish practice.

Living the Word

How would you feel about the following newspaper headline?

"Man stoned to death at edge of town for gathering firewood on a Sunday"

Who would want to put a man to death for picking up a few sticks on the Sabbath (for Jewish people, the Sabbath was Satur-

23

day, but for Christians it is Sunday). If this seems like an extreme example, be sure to read Numbers 15:32-36. Not only did a community reportedly do this to a man, but the Scripture also asserts they were simply following God's commands! What makes this particularly uncomfortable is that it assigns the death penalty to something ordinary; something nearly all of us have done. In our culture, it has not been long ago that mowing on Sunday was considered disrespectful or even forbidden. But really, the death penalty for mowing or gathering up a few sticks?

In our society we put people who are on death row in a different category; they are nothing like the rest of us who are free. They have been condemned to death for extreme wrongdoing. The majority of citizens in our society, and the laws of the land, say that what they did was so terrible they should forfeit the right to live. We are guilty of rank-ordering sinfulness. We who only lie when it is convenient and only gossip when it is about people we don't like think that we are more easily forgiven than murderous predators or those who bring shame on themselves when their adultery is reported in the news media.

Yet in the Sermon on the Mount (see Matthew 5–7) Jesus taught that there is no difference, in God's sight, between the act of adultery and merely looking at a woman or man with lust. There is no difference between murder and cursing one's brother or sister "in the heart." In short, all sins separate us from God, and to be separated from God is death. God is the giver of life, and when we turn away, intentionally or unintentionally, sin of any variety separates us from God, and that means death.

The bad news is that we are all guilty of sin. Possibly those of us who think we are not "severely sinful" are in the most jeopardy, for we think we might be good enough to pass, to make it on our own. But let's be clear: Sin results in death. Period. We are on spiritual death row, and the only hope we have is God's mercy, God's desire to forgive us.

The good news is that Jesus came, like the sacrificial lamb, to take away the sins of the world, not just the sins of bad people, but also the sins of those of us who think we are pretty good already.

Let us pray:
Lord, have mercy on us. Forgive us for judging others. Instead, help us to rejoice in the new life that you have given us in Christ. Amen.

When Tasks Overwhelm

Hearing the Word

Psalm 119, the longest of the one hundred fifty psalms, is a long, carefully structured poem about the law of the Lord. For the Israelites, the Law was more than the Ten Commandments. The Law, generally speaking, refers to the Torah, the first five books of the Bible. While there are clearly some laws and religious rules contained in those books, the majority of the material is not written in "law" form. However, lessons can be learned from the history contained in those books, and they certainly serve to teach the importance of keeping the laws of God. Both this psalm and the lesson scripture today (King David instructs his son Solomon to keep following God's laws) point out that it is important to learn and obey God's law.

Living the Word

The laws in Illinois let fifteen-year-olds have a permit to learn to drive a car. Then, at the tender age of sixteen, the child gets the keys. I remember being plenty mature to handle driving at age fourteen. I remember that I could not wait to be fifteen, and then sixteen, when I would be all grown up! Now I'm a father, and my oldest son has his permit. It is amazing how much younger fifteen is now, a generation later!

One good thing, though, is that between then and now Illinois has added a new requirement. The child—and I use that word quite intentionally—has to complete twenty-five hours of driving under the supervision of a parent before receiving a driver's license. The parent must sign a chart listing the date and times of all twenty-five hours, note the driving conditions, and so forth. I think it is a great plan. It gives me twenty-five hours to talk to my son about safe driving, and I'm taking advantage of every minute. What I want him to learn, more than the mere skills of operating the automobile, is an inner acceptance of the laws that are meant to help him and others. I hope he will come to appreciate the laws instead of see them as a challenge to break without getting caught. For while there are no guarantees about anything out there on the road, those who reject the laws are more likely to suffer the consequences than those who try to obey the laws during their driving career. And one of the groups most notorious for breaking the rules are boys between the ages of sixteen and eighteen.

Like any set of rules, the rules of the road could feel oppressive. A policeman told me that one day he pulled over a minister who was not wearing a seat belt. When the pastor was told it was the law that he wear it, the pastor argued that it was not a just law, and told the policeman it violated his rights to make choices. Further, he said that he had preached the same message to his congregation. At that, the policeman had a little talk with the pastor in the squad car. He said he told the pastor that in Scripture it says to obey the laws of the land as well as God's laws. Apparently it worked. The pastor apologized and said he had never thought about it that way. His authority was God, and the pastor had resented what he felt to be an "outside" intrusion. When the policeman reinterpreted the law as being God's will too, that made the pastor want to keep it.

Like the laws of most states that tell us to buckle up, God's laws are given for our good. They are meant to protect our social order and us. To keep them is no guarantee that everything will always be rosy, but it is the best road map to a wholesome, happy life. When we ignore God's laws, it is at our own peril.

Let us pray:
Thank you, God, for caring enough about us to teach us your ways. You could turn us loose in the world without any rules or guidance, but instead you have taught any who will listen the road to a good life. Help us gladly learn your ways and practice them in our daily life. Amen.

When Goals Are Reached

Hearing the Word

The Israelites lived too far away from the Temple in Jerusalem to worship there very often. Therefore it was common for them to make trips to the Temple only for special religious festivals and holy days. This psalm captures the feeling of longing to be at such a special and important place. It is touching that the writer takes time to notice the birds that built their nests in the protection of the Temple (if you have ever seen massive buildings, you know it is common for birds to find the protection of high ornamental stonework to be attractive nesting sites). Further, the psalm implies that just as the birds find their true home at the Temple, it is the place where the psalmist truly feels at home too.

Living the Word

If you could go back and visit any place from your past, where would you go? For some people, it might be a cabin on a Wisconsin lake where year after year Mom and Dad relaxed and spent quality time with the family. It might be a zoo or a professional ballpark you visited regularly enough to believe you knew everything about that place. It might be a tree house you and your childhood friends built by a stream in the woods. Perhaps it is the house where you lived your happiest formative years. Or it may be your "home" church—the place where you could run around in fellowship hall and smell coffee and hear the talk of adults and eat fifty vanilla wafers before the potluck lunch got underway, the place where you explored your life goals in youth meetings, the place where you eventually got married.

Wherever that special place is for you, what makes it so special? What feelings does thinking about it evoke? Chances are there are many happy memories associated with such a place. Just being there is therefore an experience. It is like being bathed in happiness and a past that is safe, affirming, and wholesome. Probably that happened not merely because of the rustic setting or the architecture. The positive feelings first come from the people whom you associate with that place.

In Psalm 84, the writer's longing to be at the Temple is rooted in the fellowship of the people and in spending time in the special presence of God. The details of the psalmist's memory even include the birds that nest there, something a child would be likely to notice, and which for adults becomes one of the treasured parts of the experience of being there.

Some children do not get to come to church very often. Their parents spend Sunday mornings doing other things, so the "special places" for these children become something other than the church and its fellowship. That seems like a real loss, for what better "special home of the heart" could we have than being in God's presence?

Fortunately, children are often pretty open to coming to Sunday school and church even if their parents sleep in or work or just stay too busy for church. That means churches can do something truly significant for the children of their community. They can invite and offer to bring the children to church often. To do so gives the child the special gift of making the church one of the safe and wholesome treasured spots of that child's memory. Later in life it is a vital seed that is likely to take root.

There are many occasions when, as adults, we long to be "back home," wherever and whatever that means to us. It is truly a valuable gift when we can help a child grow up with the feeling that the church is a place just as important as the zoo, or a fishing spot, or a tree house next to a stream. The church should be a place of safety, of warmth, and of love, and a place where we feel right at home in God's presence.

Let us pray:
Thank you for helping us feel at home in your church. Thank you for all those who, through loving me and making me feel accepted, have made the church a welcoming place to be. Open our eyes today to see the children who are growing up in our midst without the benefit of feeling the warmth and acceptance of a family of faith. Use each of us to offer an invitation and a warm welcome, and help us make our church a place the children will always rejoice to call home. Amen.

READ IN YOUR BIBLE: *Nahum 1:2-8*

SUGGESTED PSALM: *Psalm 77*

SUGGESTED HYMNS:

"*How Firm a Foundation*" (*All*)

"*Immortal, Invisible, God Only Wise*" (*B, E, F, L, P, UM, W*)

When Compromise Ruins

Hearing the Word

The short book of Nahum was written to rejoice over the fall of Nineveh, the capital city of Assyria, and to interpret that historical event as a case of God's punishment against Israel's enemy. For two hundred fifty years, the mighty Assyrians had attacked and victimized Israel. The Northern Kingdom fell to the Assyrians in 721 B.C., although the Southern Kingdom of Judah, including Jerusalem, survived (only to fall to Assyria's successors, the Babylonians, in 586 B.C.). It is interesting that in the book of Jonah, Nineveh is the city to which Jonah was sent. It is understandable that he ran from the task of carrying the Lord's message to the capital city of his country's enemy! Yet in that book his preaching worked; all Nineveh repented, and God spared them.

The books of Jonah and Nahum are not mutually exclusive. Jonah was written as a parable, and could certainly have been written many years before the historical events that led to Nahum's prophecy. Still, the two books together reflect both Israel's understandable joy at the fall of a brutal enemy (a wish even expressed by Jonah, who whined when God spared Nineveh), and their concept of the broadness of God's mercy, that it might even apply to an enemy like Nineveh.

Living the Word

A few of Hollywood's chase scenes have ended with some variation of a clever dilemma that goes something like this: The "bad guy" of the movie falls over the railing on the 100th floor of a hotel, but manages to catch hold of a pole. Dangling precariously in space, the evil villain, who moments ago would have shot the hero with glee, now pleads for the hero to save his life. Given the violence and heartless mayhem the criminal has caused up to that point in the movie, simple justice would suggest that the best coarse of action would be to shout, "Look out below!", stomp on his fingers, and then go have a nice meal to celebrate.

On the other hand, in movies that fall into other categories, the hero is likely to grasp the hand of the villain, and even though the rascal goes to jail, his life is at least spared. After all, a true hero has mercy and grace, even beyond the demands of justice.

These two basic storylines are found in American literature and films because they reflect our divergent thoughts and feelings about the larger story of life. One school of thought is that God will destroy everyone who is evil. The other school of thought is that God is so merciful that God will rescue even those who do not deserve to be rescued. So, what is God really like? Nahum seems to be a vote for finger-stomping and even celebrating about it! Jonah, by contrast, paints the picture of a God who goes to incredible lengths to reach out the hand of grace and mercy to the same city, Nineveh.

It is tempting to be in a rush to explain away either the judgment or the grace of God. For example, someone might say, "First, God used Jonah to show mercy to the people of Nineveh; but when that didn't work, God destroyed them." In other words, God's grace is only temporary; God's punishment is eternal. But is that what you believe? If it is, let's hope you are a quick learner and able to overcome all of your sins on the first or second try!

A strong case can be made from biblical examples that God's punishment is meant to educate and motivate us to be true followers; it is not meant to be an end in itself. So like a loving parent who must use discipline to teach a child the right way to live, God uses punishment as one means to a grace-filled end. We should not be in a rush to deny God's judgment, nor to shortchange God's mercifulness. Both the scent of heaven and the fear of hell can motivate people to do God's will.

Let us pray:
O God of judgment and God of mercy, we humbly ask your forgiveness for the ways we have sinned against you and our neighbor. In large ways and small we have turned our backs on you. Guide us, reshape our lives, and forgive us, for we pray in the name of Jesus Christ, the one who lived a life of love and mercy. Amen.

READ IN YOUR BIBLE: *Isaiah 40:1-5* December 3, 2000
SUGGESTED PSALM: *Psalm 66*
SUGGESTED HYMNS:
  "O Come, O Come, Emmanuel" (B, E, F, L, P, UM, W)
  "Joy to the World" (All)

Preparing for Christ's Birth

Hearing the Word

Isaiah 40 marks a new beginning in the book of Isaiah. In the thirty-nine chapters before it, Isaiah was busy confronting the Israelites about their sinfulness and warning them that they needed to change. But then disaster came upon them in the form of the Babylonian Exile in 586 B.C. Isaiah 40 and the following chapters address that historical situation, one in which the people needed God's comfort and felt that God had abandoned God's promise to the people. The urge to "prepare" for God's coming is a theme that John the Baptist echoed in advance of Jesus' ministry in the New Testament.

Living the Word

Whether you realize it or like it, countless stores and businesses have been preparing for you for months. In the gift industry, for example, the porcelain Santa figurines and metal angel candlesticks begin to ship to retailers in August for the "Christmas buying season." However, in order to be shipped in August, the products must be manufactured in the few months prior; that means the customers (local retail stores) must place their initial orders at the major trade shows and through the catalogs as early as January for the following Christmas—that is eleven months in advance! But that is not all. In order for retail stores to have new merchandise to choose from, the manufacturers have been planning new lines, testing the market, and developing specific products for Christmas at least six to eight months before the January trade shows begin. So when you walk into a store this December and see the merchandise and hear the electronic Christmas carols, just be aware that even though you may have just realized you needed to buy a gift for Aunt Gertrude, the stores have been preparing for this moment for the past eighteen months.

Further, they have prepared your mind for Christmas, to some extent. Through their advertising, they have planted certain thoughts in your mind. For example, (1) Christmas is a time to buy presents for other people, and to let other people know what gifts you might like to receive; (2) certain items are highly desirable as gifts; and (3) a particular store is the best place to find the gifts you need to buy. In short, the business world has prepared your mind to accept the idea that you need to buy in order to celebrate.

But how can we prepare for Christmas? Some prepare by enrolling in a Christmas payroll-reduction savings program, filling the valleys of the Christmas fund with cash ready to spend. Some prepare by finally paying off the credit cards from last year's Christmas. So, financially, we often make preparations for Christmas too. They may not equal the scope of preparations that businesses make for consumers, but in some way both sides typically prepare for the Christmas buying spree.

Halt! Does this preparation have anything to do with Advent? Wouldn't it be great if the same amount of time and thought and energy went into preparing for Christmas spiritually? Instead of a little swell in church attendance in the week or two before Christmas, there would be people just pouring in the doors all year long! It would be just as hard to find a parking place at church as it is at the mall! And what if everyone simply gave the Bible equal time with catalogs and sale ads? Surely some of the things in the Bible would rub off, and our minds would be just as full of "good news that Christ is born" as "good news of great sales." Perhaps we as a nation would donate the same amount of money, in an act of reckless generosity, to fight world hunger as we do to purchase material things in the fourth quarter of the year!

Christmas is coming soon. May the Lord find our hearts ready to receive him.

Let us pray:

Dear Lord, forgive us for spending so much time and energy worrying about material things, not just at Christmas but all year long. Instead, fill our hearts with your presence, and help us live in a way that honors you. In Jesus' name, Amen.

SUGGESTED HYMNS:
  "It Came Upon a Midnight Clear" (All)
  "Angels We Have Heard on High" (B, E, F, L, P, UM, W)

Obeying God's Call

Hearing the Word

Today's devotional scripture, Matthew 1:18-25, is one of those famous passages we feel that we almost do not need to read; we already know what it says. However, when compared to today's lesson scripture, Luke 1:26-38, the pair give new insight. Both passages begin with the birth story of Jesus. However, Matthew tells the story from Joseph's point of view, and Luke from Mary's point of view. This may be due in part to the fact that Matthew is the more "Jewish" of the two Gospels, and thus more concerned with tracing the descendants of Jesus through the male ancestors. In any case, it is interesting to compare the two stories, the two announcements, and the two ways Mary and Joseph were affected by the news of a baby coming to them, according to their culture and their plans, far too early. In the end, even though Mary and Joseph had questions about the plan, both complied to what they felt was God's will for them.

Living the Word

One of the more creative suggestions for how to handle stress: Put a paper grocery bag over your head and put a sign on it that says, "Closed for remodeling."

Both Mary and Joseph must have had some stress about having a baby. And both of them needed a little "remodeling" done to their thoughts as a result.

Let's begin with Mary. She was minding her own business when suddenly an angel appeared to her and said, "Peace be with you!" Angels are peaceful creatures, at least in movies. Still, it is bound to raise the blood pressure a notch or two when one actually appears at your side and talks to you. So, already the stress had begun for Mary. What would you think about your own state of mind if you saw an angel? Who would you want to tell?

Conversation ensued, and unfortunately, it was not exactly the solution for stress. (If you want peace on earth, having a baby is not the fastest way to that goal, not to mention having one in that society out of wedlock!) Mary was right on target to wonder whether she could be pregnant, since she was still a virgin. But the angel helped her realize that with God, anything is possible. That was just the "remodeling" she needed. She was about to say yes to one of the greatest moments in history.

Mary did not have much choice but to tell Joseph. At least she had the experience of seeing the angel to lean on, but he hadn't. He simply heard his fiancée tell him she was pregnant, and he knew it wasn't by him. One wonders how smoothly the conversation went between the two, but that is not recorded in the Bible. All we know is that Joseph did not believe Mary's story. He simply had to deal with what he perceived to be her betrayal, lies to cover it up, their reputations, plus, of course, a baby on the way. Clearly, he was under stress, and his thoughts needed some remodeling too.

Martin Luther once commented that there are three miracles of Christmas: (1) God came to earth; (2) a virgin had a baby; and (3) Mary believed. And the greatest miracle, he said, was that Mary believed.

It was a miracle, and it still is a miracle, when God can change our minds, change our way of looking at life. It is easy to be stressed out by the events of life, but part of Christmas should be the remodeling of our minds, so that the greatest miracle can happen all over again. Sometimes we need to look beyond the obvious for God at work. God may not always work the way we expect, and many times God is quite busy at work in the interruptions of our lives and in the changes in our plans.

Yes, it is a miracle that God came to dwell on earth, and it is a miracle that a virgin could have a baby. But if we could just be ready to see God's will and believe like Mary and Joseph, that would be one of the greatest miracles of Christmas.

Let us pray:

Lord, I believe. And yet help me in spite of my unbelief, so that I may see your hand at work in my life and be ready to do your will. Amen.

Praising God

Hearing the Word

The three verses of today's devotional scripture reading are words of thanksgiving that are typical of Old Testament praise. They are reminiscent of Mary's song of praise, known as the Magnificat, after she learned that she was to bear God's Son. That provides the link between the devotional text (Psalm 34:1-3) and the lesson text for today (Luke 1:39-56). Psalm 34 does not remain strictly in a praise mode; it continues by comparing the fate of good people and evil people. The instructional nature of this psalm is characteristic of the "wisdom psalms." Incidentally, Psalm 34 is also written as an acrostic, which means that each line begins with a different letter of the Hebrew alphabet, arranged in alphabetical order.

Living the Word

Two friends had hunted together for years, but one was frustrated that no matter what happened, all his friend would do was complain, criticize, and bemoan the negative things in life. He tried to show his friend how to issue a compliment by saying nice things to him whenever he accomplished something, but nothing seemed to jar his friend out of his negativity. One day he purchased a new hunting dog and soon discovered that it was truly special. Instead of jumping in and swimming to retrieve ducks on the water, it would actually run across the top of the water without getting wet! He couldn't wait to show his new dog to his sullen friend.

One day they went hunting ducks together. Soon the moment came for his new dog to go get a duck. After the dog ran across the water and back, the hunter turned proudly to his pessimistic friend. Fully expecting some enthusiasm, wonder, or at least a kind remark, he asked, "Well, did you notice anything unusual about my new hunting dog?" "Yeah," muttered the friend, "He can't swim."

If you work hard enough at it, you can always avoid the positive side of life. You can always avoid giving God praise for all that God has done. Someone once commented, "There is just enough light in the world for those who want to see, and just enough darkness in the world for those with a contrary disposition." A true pessimist will always notice that the glass is half empty, or at least until it spills. Then they will rise up and complain that glass was half full!

Praise is really not that painful, however. In fact, it feels good! It is therapeutic to recognize our gifts and cultivate a thankful heart. After Mary learned about the birth of Jesus, she uttered (or maybe sang) some of the Bible's most beautiful words of praise. Likewise, Psalm 34 begins with what is probably a hymn of praise, even though it is primarily a teaching psalm.

Who is the last person you gave a sincere, heartfelt compliment to? When was the last time you publicly praised someone you care about, particularly a child or spouse? Praise is to the human heart what rain is to the parched desert. The difference is that the desert has to wait for the weather; but when it comes to praising other people, what are you waiting for? Rain in the desert?

The same holds true for praising God. God is so good to us; every day is filled with blessings. So often we are like those who don't know if the trees are bare or flowering, because we walk with downcast eyes. Let us lift up our eyes, see all that God is doing, and give God praise. Then make it your goal in life to find something good in every person you meet, and say a kind word about that good thing. If you look at life with faith and gratitude, you will learn to overlook the fact that the hunting dog can't swim, and notice how well it walks on water!

Let us pray:
Lord, wipe the scowls off our faces and take away the pangs of worry and doubt. Open our eyes to behold your precious gifts, and make room in our heart today for praise and joy. In the name of Jesus, who came to give us life in all its abundance. Amen.

SUGGESTED PSALM: *Psalm 96*

SUGGESTED HYMNS:

"*Silent Night*" *(All)*

"*O Little Town of Bethlehem*" *(All)*

Welcoming the Savior

Hearing the Word

Peter's declaration about Jesus at Caesarea Philippi was a pivotal moment in Jesus' ministry. It marked the first time that one of the disciples "figured it out" and made such a bold declaration of faith about Jesus. In a sense, it was a turning point between Jesus' teaching and redemptive missions, too. While Jesus taught and healed throughout his earthly ministry, these activities were apparently the focus of his work up until Caesarea Philippi. Afterward, Jesus spoke of his coming suffering and death; and the movement toward Jerusalem begins in Matthew, Mark, and Luke.

Here, on Christmas Eve, the devotional scripture is tied to the lesson scripture (the birth story of Jesus) because the angels declared to the shepherd in the fields that "To you is born this day in the city of David a Savior, who is the Messiah, the Lord" (Luke 2:11).

Living the Word

In an 1876 memo, a company executive commented on a new invention called the "telephone." His analysis of the newfangled idea was that the device had too many shortcomings, no future, and was of no value to the company. Ironically, the person who wrote the memo worked for a company that we know today as a telecommunications giant! Evidently, somebody in that company saw the value of the telephone. They ignored that executive's proclamation, and the rest is history.

Can you imagine life without the telephone? In some ways, it is a pleasant thought—particularly on days when the phone won't quit ringing. We have come to depend on it as a vital business and personal tool. Today, many people have multiple phone lines both at work and at home. Not only do we have a phone number, but also a fax number, a mobile phone number, a beeper number, and an e-mail address. For better or for worse, the phone has made us more accessible to one another. In a way, the birth of Christ is like the invention of the telephone. Angels proclaimed the importance of his birth, and his parents knew. Still, his advent did not get the attention and respect it should have, either at his birth or throughout his life. His parents had to stay in a stable with the animals, in spite of Mary's condition! If you've ever had a bad hotel experience and complained about it later, then sorry, Mary and Joseph's story really tops most others. But it was not a time of complaining; it was a night of joy. Even though many people were oblivious to the birth of the Savior of the world, and others dismissed the birth as an everyday event, a few people understood the importance of that baby and celebrated. The shepherds, the wise men, and of course, Mary and Joseph celebrated Jesus' birth. Happily, others soon recognized how important Jesus' birth and life was to the world; and today, it is easily true that no one life has ever made as much historical and spiritual difference than the life of Jesus Christ.

The advent of the telephone changed the world and created bridges between people. In a much more important way, the advent of Jesus changed the world and created a bridge between God and humanity. Because Jesus was born, we can really talk with God as a friend, and not as someone distant and unknown.

This Christmas, pick up the phone and call someone you love who lives in a distant place. But as you dial the number, say a quick prayer of thanks to God for the gift of Jesus Christ, who opened up the lines of communication even without a phone line.

Let us pray:

Thank you, Lord, for the birth of Jesus Christ. Thank you for the difference Jesus has made in my life and to the lives of so many others. Help me keep the lines of communication open with you, Lord, that I may know your will and celebrate this special and holy event. Amen.

READ IN YOUR BIBLE: *Isaiah 52:7-10*   **December 31, 2000**
SUGGESTED PSALM: *Psalm 146*
SUGGESTED HYMNS:
   "What Child Is This" (B, E, F, L, P, UM, W)
   "While Shepherds Watched Their Flocks" (B, C, E, F, P, UM, W)

Recognizing the Christ

Hearing the Word

These beautiful words from Isaiah come at a bleak time in Israel's history. Those who survived the crushing defeat of Judah (along with the destruction of the Temple in Jerusalem) were forced into exile in Babylonia. The feelings of the Israelites might not be far removed from the feelings of the refugees who fled Kosovo in the spring of 1999. Like those refugees, the Israelites had lost their homes, their loved ones, and their identity. Imagine their thirst for some good news; the hope that the war would give way to peace and the chance to return home. Isaiah paints this picture of hope for the Israelites, and bases this vision not on mere wistfulness, but on the future work of God.

Living the Word

As of this writing, there are now about 1.5 million refugees who have fled Kosovo. Most of the refugees are women, children, and older people. It is becoming apparent that in village after village, many of the young and middle-aged men have been rounded up and shot. Many of the women have been raped, many of their homes have been burned, and all of the refugees who survived have been stripped of their money, possessions, and legal documents. Many children have been orphaned or lost in the violence. One little girl, shown on a news report, had followed a family of strangers at a distance for two days; they finally realized she had no family in that group of refugees, so they took her in. She could not speak, so they named her after the village they think she came from. The pathetic reports go on and on. That's war. Isaiah first wrote to address the pain and suffering of the Israelites.

We see it on the news every day; the stories may change, but the face of loss and grief changes little. The details could be a savage hurricane, or a string of killer tornadoes, or a school bus crash, or a gunman's deadly rampage, or a car bomb. Human misery is not difficult to visualize. Positive outcomes to these situations are more difficult to visualize. For example, when three U.S. soldiers were captured, plenty of people speculated that they might be given an unjust trial, mistreated in prison, or even tortured. That is one vision. But the people who succeeded in obtaining freedom for the soldiers were a delegation of church people. They held onto a vision of the soldiers coming home, free and unhurt. Then they acted on that vision.

Of course no human being can know what the future holds. Here on the last day of the famous year 2000, nobody can see what 2001 will hold. Yet one of the great gifts that the church has to offer the world is the hope of a brighter vision for tomorrow. When someone is suffering, it is encouraging and wholesome merely to think about a positive resolution. For example, the sick person who thinks about what it will be like when he/she recovers has an important attitudinal edge over the person who feels certain that there is no hope.

Isaiah wrote about hope. He helped the suffering and lost people of Israel have hope again. The hope he offered was not based on a whim or speculation. It was based on knowing that God was on their side and that God was there to love and support the people. If you were to peek ahead at the end of the story for the year 2001, and for the rest of your life, do you have some hope today? Ultimately our hope truly rests in God.

Some people face the future with worry, or even dread. And some people have legitimate fears about their future. But Christians should hold out hope in the world. In the midst of pain and grief, it truly is refreshing to see one coming to be with you who has a light step and brings hope everywhere she or he may go.

Let us pray:
Lord, help us to be people of hope. Help us start more sentences with the words "I hope" rather than the words "I doubt if." Especially when those around us are losing their ability to keep hope alive, help us to be people of hope. In the name of Jesus Christ, the true hope of the world. Amen.

Discovering Your Mission

Hearing the Word

Isaiah 61 is probably most famous for being the scripture Jesus chose to describe his mission on earth. When he selected a scripture to read and speak about in his hometown synagogue just before beginning his public ministry, Jesus chose the first three verses of this passage, then said that the scripture was fulfilled even as the people heard it being read. The lesson scripture today (Luke 4:16-30) records this event, linking the two passages together. Interestingly, Jesus' mission seemed to be to help the outcast of society, and soon after he read this scripture and commented about it, he became an outcast too. The people of his hometown became angry with him and even tried to kill him. Jesus left town, and his ministry was begun.

Living the Word

A famous person, invited back to speak at his alma mater high school graduation, refused to attend the event. He remarked that he never felt accepted when he went to school there, so why should he accept their "fair-weather" friendship now? His attitude hurt and angered some people in that community, but it should make us all think about whom we accept and why.

In childhood games we must learn to deal with acceptance and rejection as well as choose whom to accept and whom to reject. Children "choose up sides" for a ball game. The last person to be chosen often experiences humiliation. "Nobody wanted me." That is a harsh feeling for a child.

Teens must struggle with courtship and acceptance by their peers. What do you have to do to be "in"? If you are not "in," then

41

you are, in a sense, outcast. That is a painful feeling for teens. Many teens in every town must deal with rejection and feeling like an outsider. They may not attend your church or all of the ball games at school. They may stay home a lot and not participate in many extracurricular activities. Have you made an opportunity to get to know one or more kids like that in your community? Could you? Would you take a step in that direction this week, somehow?

In every community there are those whose lives have been filled with rejection. They may have become alcoholic, been rejected by spouse and children, lost their job, and felt unacceptable to society in general. It is also true for some people who live in poverty, or who face certain health problems, or whose criminal past is well known, or who have a handicapping condition. Even "strange" thoughts can cause others to distance themselves from us. That is how Jesus came to be cast out, literally, from this hometown. As long as he was a local carpenter's son, he was acceptable. But when he started to talk like he thought he might be the Messiah, then they would not accept him. There are many people in every town who, for a variety of reasons, are made to feel like outcasts just like Jesus.

That is why it is important for us to remember Jesus' mission statement, Isaiah 61. Jesus came to bring good news to the downtrodden, the prisoners, the poor, and the outcast. The good news, of course, is that God loves and accepts them too. Jesus then lived his life in a way that demonstrated just how much they were loved. The angels did not go to the religious officials, but to the shepherds outside of town. Jesus noticed the people that the "socially accepted ones" overlook and reject. Jesus even ate with sinners such as prostitutes and tax collectors.

There is a little outcast in most of us, particularly if we take sin seriously. Sin makes us unacceptable to God, so that we would have no hope of being invited to the feast in the kingdom of God. But Jesus came into the world to announce that in God's family all are invited. All are a part. With God, you are accepted.

Let us pray:
Lord, thank you for coming into the world to change us from God's enemies to God's friends; thank you for noticing the outsider and for inviting me to your joyous feast. Help me watch for those who are not included in my community, and work through my life to grant your hospitality and love to others. In Jesus' name, Amen.

READ IN YOUR BIBLE: *Matthew 10:34-39*   **January 14, 2001**

SUGGESTED PSALM: *Psalm 122*

SUGGESTED HYMNS:

"*Stand Up, Stand Up for Jesus*" (B, C, E, F, L, UM)

"*Lift High the Cross*" (B, L, P, UM, W)

Counting the Cost

Hearing the Word

Traditional Judaism builds a society and the strength of the nation on the foundation of loyalty to one's family. As Paul pointed out in Ephesians 6:1-3, the commandment to honor father and mother is the first one with a promise, and that promise is "that it may be well with you . . . on the earth." Thus, for Jesus to elevate devotion to God above devotion to family indicates how radical it is to put God first. Not only that, but most people hold their own life in high esteem; Jesus, though, indicated that our loyalty to God must supersede even our loyalty to our own life. All of this is a way of underlining how vital it is to put God first, not to say that Christians cannot get along with their families.

Living the Word

Placing a high value on family time should not conflict with placing a high value on church time, normally. However, sometimes clergy hear people make statements that assume a conflict between family and church. Here are some examples:

"*I can't come to church this week because that is the only day we have for family time.*" Unfortunately, this excuse creates a conflict where there should be none. Our faith and the church community should be powerful assets on the side of holding families together—and helping them through difficult times too. Going to church is great family time.

"*Since our visiting relatives are not coming to church, I feel like I need to stay home with them.*" Many pastors nod understandingly when they hear this excuse, and they let the person off the hook. Yet if Jesus meant what he said in today's challenging scripture lesson,

43

he probably would not nod understandingly. He might point out that some conflicts are worthwhile. Yes, it would create a conflict if the host couple leave the house and abandon the guests who refuse to come with them to church, leaving them unfed and alone in the house. It is not very hospitable, but it would make a statement about how vital church is to the hosts. Further, it could even result in a whole pew full of members, plus another pew full of visitors, being there instead of two empty pews.

Other legitimate conflicts can occur that pit our loyalty to God against our loyalty to our family. For example, religious differences are often brought into a marriage. One spouse thinks it is important to have the new baby baptized, while the other strongly advocates "believer's baptism" when the child is old enough to understand the meaning of baptism. Or perhaps one spouse does not believe in God at all, while the other one wants to take the children to Sunday school.

Such conflicts often do not have easy answers. For example, how does today's scripture relate to the couple who differs on whether to baptize the baby? Both, after reading Jesus' words, might well say "I see that my religious duties are more important than my loyalty to my family." So one will use this argument to show how important it is to have the baby baptized, even if it disregards the wish of the spouse; the other spouse will be reinforced in the decision to wait to have the baby baptized! Real life is usually more complicated and messy than the "rules" often sound. Surely Jesus did not mean to introduce harshness and difficulty into our lives with this teaching. Instead, conflict is already there; difficult decisions and value struggles are part of family life and religious life.

This is one of the "difficult" teachings of Jesus. But when it is seen positively, it simply means that God should be first in our life. We may love our life and other people intensely, but God's love for us, if we can imagine it, is even stronger and more lasting than any human love could ever be.

Let us pray:
Help us love our family members more, not in competition with our loyalty to you, but because of our commitment to you. Help us come to understand that no matter how strong our love may be for any person or thing, your love for us is stronger still. In Jesus' name we pray, Amen.

Celebrating Reconciliation

Hearing the Word

The devotional scripture lesson for today ends at Ephesians 2:2, although theologically it would be nice to continue until at least the end of verse 5. As verse 2 ends, Paul is still describing spiritual death, but verses 4 and 5 get around to the subject of God bringing us back to life through Christ. The idea of spiritual death and resurrection is expressed in a story Jesus told about the prodigal son (which is the lesson scripture for today). For the apostle Paul, God's grace, and not keeping the law, was the only thing that gives us any hope of new life with God. Spiritual death is a natural condition and an inevitable result of our sin, which is also inevitable without God. Only God's powerful mercy can spare us from the inevitability of this cycle of sin and death.

Living the Word

A *National Geographic* article explored the world of ants and observed that, for tiny insects, ants are incredibly well organized and seemingly smart! For example, a colony can form a relationship with a certain kind of plant in order to exploit the desirable liquids that plant produces. Tiny ant "guards" are posted in key positions around the plant and will defend it to the death. Obviously, this is good for the plant, because the ants keep away bugs with piggish appetites for leaves.

The writer of the article, at points, seemed to imply that the plants produce this liquid just for this one purpose—like it was the plant's plan, though surely the writer would not say that plants, even smart ones, make plans. After all, what plant first woke up one morning with the bright idea, "Hey, if I can just make some sweet stuff and get those ants marching by to taste it, I think they'll like it, form a colony right here, and keep these nasty caterpillars from chewing my leaves to bits." No, that would be silly! It must have been the ants' idea!

One of the great contributions of science is to open our eyes to the purely miraculous world around us. Most of us see an ant and think about getting a newspaper to swat it, or maybe feel guilty for frying one with a magnifying glass as a kid. Our relationship with them isn't all that great. But those tiny animals, if you spend the time to study them, are nothing short of miracles walking around on six tiny legs. Some of them actually "milk" aphids and babysit them. Others work in huge team efforts to pull distant leaves into a bundle to create a nesting spot high in the trees. Who tells them when to pull, where to stand, and how to cooperate in a colony of fifty thousand? Who first helped them figure out that a leaf one ant could never budge, a hundred pulling together could move into place?

Remember, we are just talking about ants here—tiny pests at picnics to most folks! Yet if you open your eyes to them, it is not too difficult to see God's miraculous hand at work, God's love for all the creatures, and God's providence even to the smallest detail.

The apostle Paul speaks of the great power that is at work in our lives when we let God work in us. He points to the resurrection of Christ and to the power that God has in order to accomplish it, then Paul tells us that this is the same powerful God who is working in us. The power of God can be seen in the Resurrection and in the wonders of nature. It is inspiring to have our eyes opened to the miracles of God's creation. It is wonderful to know that the same God who commanded the mighty mountains to rise up, who gently helps the butterfly emerge from the cocoon, and who created the wonderful diversity of birds, from hummingbirds to penguins to ostriches, is the same God who loves us, walks with us through life, and is at work in our hearts.

Let us pray:
Dear Lord, open our eyes to the wonders around us, that we may truly appreciate every expression of your creative power and tender love. Thank you for your work in our lives. Help us trust you to shape us and form us as you will. In Jesus' name, Amen.

SUGGESTED HYMNS:
　"*Lord, I Want to Be a Christian*" *(B, C, F, P, UM, W)*
　"*All Hail the Power of Jesus' Name*" *(All)*

Preparing for the Future

Hearing the Word

You might think that Jesus would have spoken the most about prayer or some sort of religious practice. However, one of Jesus' most frequent topics was greed and stewardship. That may be because how people handle money shows their real priorities in life; it is easy to profess love for God and neighbor, but the test is often either passed or failed when we sit down to pay the bills.

The parable of the rich fool paints an unforgettable picture. Like the wisdom teachers of Jesus' day, Jesus used a short story to illustrate a wise saying (like the moral of the story in verse 21). It also portrays the man as being 100 percent foolish. In the wisdom tradition, as a way to more clearly see the point, the contrast between wise and foolish is sharply drawn. Here there is no need to paint the picture of a wise man as a contrast; the picture of the fool is so clear that the point is made without further detail.

Living the Word

The story Jesus tells here sounds an awful lot like the retirement plans almost all of us make. We contribute to that "bigger barn" all of our life in the form of Social Security, an IRA fund, and pension accounts. The point of all that saving is to provide for that time of life when, as this scripture says, we can say to ourselves, "You have all the good things you need for many years. Take life easy, eat, drink, and enjoy yourself" (v. 19 TEV).

Two things makes this story so uncomfortable. First, it sounds entirely reasonable and prudent for this man to want a little more for retirement and to prepare for it, but Jesus is using this man as an example of a fool. Second, this man sounds exactly like us!

47

After all, Zacchaeus was a "wee little man" who climbed trees, and Goliath was a giant who was too dumb to wear protective headgear into battle. Both of those guys are different enough to make their stories comfortable. But this rich guy planning for retirement! His shoes fit our feet, and it's a perfect fit! So what is wrong with what this "foolish" man did?

Let's try to identify some of the mistakes made by the rich fool. First, he was greedy. Greed always wants a bigger barn, or boat, or yard, or house, or savings account. Greed breeds dissatisfaction with the barns that we have, for we link happiness to something we do not have.

Second, it would be ideal to spend everything and give everything away while we have life, for that means we have efficiently used all the money that comes into our control. Anything that is still invested or stuck under the mattress means that when you die, you have simply transferred the decisions about how to use it to your heirs. When people are starving to death in our world today, it can be negligent and sinful to sit on a million-dollar account and tell ourselves, "Well, that's for the future."

Third, the rich fool demonstrated a lack of faith in God's providence for the future. His foolishness was thinking about providing for his own future when he didn't even have a future! This story shows that we are not God, for we cannot provide ourselves with life. Thus, trust is misplaced unless it is put in God, and God alone.

Does all this mean it is wrong to save for retirement? Not necessarily; it is good stewardship to plan to purchase the basics of life for a time when income is less. On the other hand, saving for retirement can become so obsessive, governed by fear or greed, that it cripples our generosity in the present and our ability to make a difference now.

This scripture should remind us that the future we plan for is not a certainty, and so we should not postpone the good we can do today. Further, it may well cause us to revisit our motivations and to question how our savings plans can serve God and others as well as merely ourselves.

Let us pray:
Save us from greed, self-centeredness, and fear. Grant us hearts full of faith, love, and compassion, that we may become more generous and better stewards of the gifts you loan us for this short time. Amen.

Reclaiming the Lost

Hearing the Word

This scripture is loosely linked to others in this section of Matthew by the term "little ones." At the beginning of chapter 18, Jesus calls a child to sit before the disciples as an example that they must become like children (note that this is a different incident than "let the children come to me . . ." elsewhere in the Gospels). However, the other references to "little ones" should not presume children only. In Matthew 18:6-9, "little ones" refers to new Christians or impressionable people and the harm of misleading them. Then, in this parable the "little ones" are the lost, and possibly those the church overlooks and ignores. It stresses the importance of noticing and seeking those we consider to be "little."

Finally, today's lesson scripture ties into this theme because Zacchaeus was a "little one" physically, but he was also "little" in his spiritual life, and "little" in the sense that the religious people had turned their backs on him and overlooked his spiritual lostness.

Living the Word

Before you set aside this devotional reading, please commit to an ongoing experiment. Pretend your life depended on you finding a way for your church to bring ten new people into the fold.

First, it might be a good idea to leave the ninety-nine and go looking for the one. That's in the Bible, and it makes good sense. Of course it is possible that the lost one will wander back into the fold, but logically, your chances of finding the lost one are better somewhere outside the church. Does that sound reasonable enough?

So get in the car, or better, take a walk. If you see an opportunity, when it is appropriate, strike up a conversation with someone you see out walking or in a store. Tell that person you have been thinking about the church, what it does and doesn't offer to people in the area, and wondering if there are things it could be doing to be helpful to other people. Then listen nondefensively to whatever ideas and/or feelings you hear. Could they benefit from a child care center, Saturday evening worship, a parent's resource center, older adult outings, an after-school "latchkey" program, a space for evening tutoring, hospitality for community events, opportunities to participate in people-to-people style local mission projects? If your church gave away free children's Bibles to kids in the neighborhood, would that have any value? Just listen carefully for what life is like and how your church can become a part of helping them make their life better by drawing closer to Christ.

This experiment is, in a word, "straying" outside of our usual daily routine in an attempt to experience people that are not part of our usual flock. There are risks associated with leaving the ninety-nine, which for most of us represents the safety we feel in our established groups and routine social contacts. But evangelism means leaving the ninety-nine to see if we can find the one that is lost. This dilemma is true for both ministers and laity, all of whom should be evangelists everywhere.

One final note about motivation: We should pursue the search as though our lives do depend on it. Why? The answer is, there are lives at stake—theirs. Unless, of course, you believe that the lost one is not in too much stress or duress as a result of being lost. If our faith, our church, and our Lord really does not make that much of a difference, then don't bother looking. Just "take care of your own" at church, and let the lost fend for themselves. Maybe Jesus did not really mean for us to read too much into this parable. Or did he?

Let us pray:
Forgive us, O Lord, for all of our excuses that stand in the way of our search for your precious lost ones in the world. Remind us that your love and your church is for everyone. Open our eyes to every opportunity to be responsive to the human need around us, hospitable especially to people that feel unworthy and outcast, and inviting to every person who needs you in their life. Amen.

SUGGESTED PSALM: *Psalm 139*
SUGGESTED HYMNS:
   "Come, We That Love the Lord" (B, C, E, F, UM, W)
   "Lord, Whose Love Through Humble Service" (E, F, L, P, UM, W)

Service: The Way to Greatness

Hearing the Word

This strange request for special privilege appears only in Matthew and Mark, and it provides an informative illustration of something scholars call the Synoptic problem. This issue has to do with the order in which the Gospels were written and the differences in narrative. This story in Mark also appears in Matthew 20:20-28, but they are not duplicate narratives. In Mark, James and John appeal directly to Jesus. In Matthew, their mother makes the appeal with the brothers silently behind her.

Why is the petitioner different? Mark is almost universally acknowledged as the earliest written Gospel. Did Matthew witness the story differently from Mark? Did Matthew have Mark's Gospel and change it for some reason. Mark's version seems to put the responsibility for the selfish request squarely on the two disciples. Matthew opens the possibility that the brothers were only acquiescing to their mother's selfish desire. But does that make them any less self-important?

Regardless the origin of the request, Jesus rebuffs it because their faith is revealed as narcissistic rather than God-centered. Furthermore, only God can determine places at the throne.

Living the Word

Once there was a rich man who had worked hard for his luxurious possessions. It deeply troubled him to think of going to heaven empty-handed, so he asked God in prayer if he could have an exception, and take some of his most cherished possessions with him. After much pleading, God finally agreed to let the man bring a single suitcase with him into heaven. Shortly before he died, he sold all of his possessions and purchased blocks of solid gold which he had specially made to fit precisely into his special suitcase. Huffing and puffing, he proceeded to heaven's gates where Saint Peter met him. "Oh," Saint Peter remarked, "You're really lucky—God doesn't usually grant that request to anybody. May I see what you decided to bring with you!"

At that, the man proudly opened his suitcase, and Saint Peter stared inside. Suddenly he looked up quizzically at the man. "You just brought pavement?"

The values of heaven are different than the values of earth. Jesus said that true greatness in heaven is seen in one who forgets the self and serves others.

True selflessness is difficult to find. We are so used to asking or wondering "What's in it for me?" Churches even use the motive to encourage donations. For example, "If you give to the church, it is tax deductible." Some Christian TV shows appeal to this motive by offering "gifts" to those who donate. Other evangelists unashamedly state that in order for God to bless you, you have to first send them money! The donation (to their ministry) "plants the seed," then God can go to work to give you abundant life! But is that a holy, heavenly reason to support a ministry—so you will get more money back?

No, in a thousand ways—in ten million ways—we put ourselves first. True selflessness, like untarnished expressions of faith, are hard to find. They are real treasures. Try to show your faith in selfless ways; these are the acts of solid gold you can fill your suitcase with and take with you anywhere, even into the Kingdom. If you are married, kiss your spouse and tell her you love her. Then do something great as a surprise. Volunteer to help underprivileged children in some capacity, but don't tell any of your friends what you are doing. Find a creative way to anonymously give a generous donation or practical gift to a person in need, such as a month's rent.

You get the idea.

Let us pray:
Help me forget about myself, Lord, and live a life of love and service, not just because it is your will, but because it is a joyous and great life. Amen.

Fulfilling One's Mission

Hearing the Word

This quarter (which consists of December, January, and February) the lesson scriptures have been exploring the story of Jesus' life as told in the Gospel of Luke. That is why, even though this is not Holy Week, we will be considering Jesus' death in this session, and Jesus' resurrection in the next. It is helpful, in order to understand the events described in this scripture, to know that the Jewish Sabbath began when the sun went down on Friday evening, and ended at sunset on Saturday evening. Also, it was not proper to handle dead bodies on the Sabbath. This explains the rush to get Jesus' body from the cross and lay him in a tomb, as the sun was about to set on Friday. It also explains why the women returned to the tomb as early as possible on Sunday morning with the embalming spices in order to care for his body, setting the stage for Easter.

Living the Word

A newspaper recently ran an advertisement from a local TV station. Due to technical difficulties, the TV station cut off the last couple of minutes of a television movie. That must have resulted in phone calls from a number of people who ranged from curious to upset. So the TV station ran the ad to apologize for cutting off the end of the movie, and to tell the end of the story.

Movies typically tell a story with a beginning, middle, and end. The time span covered in a two-hour movie can be anything from one day in someone's life to a portrait of an entire lifetime, and some historical movies even cover decades. Usually when you leave a movie, you have some feeling of resolution. The story is over. The bad guy is in jail. The misunderstandings are cleared up. The plane has miraculously landed. Even if a movie ends in death or a divorce, you usually leave understanding why it had to end that way.

In real life we do not live one storyline at a time. There are many stories which we live simultaneously; the endings and beginnings are not always neat and tidy. But we still need resolution, a sense of peace for our endings.

To illustrate the difference, consider two ways a job can end. One is to be suddenly and totally surprised by two security guards at your desk one Wednesday morning. They inform you that the company is cutting back, hand you your termination papers, wait while you pack your personal belongings, and escort you out the main gate. Compare that to another job ending: After years of faithful service to your company, you receive many gifts and out-pourings of good wishes from countless friends and fellow employees; a gold watch; a bonus check; and two tickets to a tropical resort. One ending feels like you were yanked out of the middle of the story. The other is a graceful and satisfying conclusion.

Remember that the story of Jesus' life ends when he was only thirty-three years old. That is right in the middle of a lifetime. Yet as the Gospel writers reflect on his ministry, they see that the ending that was shocking and too soon for them was, in fact, a true resolution of his earthly work. Jesus had in fact done all that he had been put on earth to do.

Some deaths and other endings are much more difficult for us to accept than others. Probably that has something to do with whether we had time to accept the outcome and to find some kind of peace and resolution to that relationship or "story" in our life. This was a most difficult and stressful ending for the disciples and the people who loved Jesus. To them, it seemed like the end of the story. What we know now, and they found out soon enough, was that with God, the endings of our lives are always the first step toward new beginnings. God's story never ends.

Let us pray:
O Lord, be with those who have been struggling this week with grief or unresolved endings in their life. Help us to walk side by side with those who suffer and mourn, holding near to our hearts the hope that all endings are, in your sight, new beginnings. In the name of Jesus, our risen Lord. Amen.

READ IN YOUR BIBLE: *Matthew 28:16-20*   **February 25, 2001**

SUGGESTED PSALM: *Psalm 148*

SUGGESTED HYMNS:

   "Praise to the Lord, the Almighty" (B, E, F, L, P, UM, W)

   "Onward Christian Soldiers" (B, C, E, F, L, UM)

You Are a Witness!

Hearing the Word

   The devotional scripture reading for today is known as the "Great Commission." It is one of the few scripture passages/events that are recorded in all four Gospels, and Acts too. Since the writer of Luke also wrote Acts, it means that the writer felt that this great commission was so important that it was worth repeating. Each Gospel writer uses different words, but they all have one thing in common; when Jesus left the disciples, he sent them into the world to continue his work.

Living the Word

   A father sent his son, a relatively new driver, out on a snowy night to pick up some items at a nearby grocery store. However, after the boy departed, the snowstorm quickly became a blizzard. The boy remembered that his dad once told him, if he were ever lost in a blizzard, to wait for a snowplow and follow it. Fortunately, a snowplow came along almost right away. For the next forty-five minutes the boy followed that plow. Finally the driver stopped, hopped down, and approached the boy's car. The boy rolled down his window and explained why he was following the plow. "Oh, that's fine, son, but I'm finished with the grocery store lot now. Do you want to follow me over to the mall?"

   At least that boy had a plan. He was trying to follow his father's directions, but unfortunately he was not getting anywhere fast. That sounds a little like the church at times. We have our heavenly Father's directions. "Go into the world and make disciples; baptize them and teach them in the name of the Father, the Son, and the Holy Spirit" (Matthew 28:16-20 paraphrased). However, there are times when our way of following Jesus' direction is about as convoluted as following a snowplow through a parking lot! How many church meetings have you attended where the main decisions, at least measured in time and emotional intensity, had to do with things that had little to do with making disciples for Jesus Christ? Examples might include things like whether to buy new Advent candles this year or use the old ones; what fabric and color to choose for the new carpet; or whether to move a special event to a different Sunday because of a school basketball game? It is true that all of these things constitute the mundane work of keeping a church going, and they must be done. And churches are fortunate when they have committed people who will spend their time to take care of needs like these. However, it is important that all Christians remember our central purpose. Our purpose is bigger than getting the "right" color for the church's carpet! It is to win disciples for Jesus Christ and teach them the Christian life.

Someone once said, "If you don't know where you are going, any road will do." The gift of the Great Commission is to give the church a clear purpose. We know what Jesus wants us to do, and can map out how to get there. For Christians, some roads are better than others, for we have a clear direction, a strong sense of purpose.

Church meetings should relate in some way to that purpose. It would not hurt a thing if the Great Commission were read as any church meeting began. Further, suppose that no church meeting could proceed until the chairperson first articulated to those in attendance how the business of that meeting relates to Jesus' Great Commission. For example, choosing carpet color can relate to the Great Commission if it helps create a hospitable environment for visitors and longtime church members too. But if ten people haggle over a carpet sample book for two hours and go home mad at each other, they may well wonder what good they have accomplished.

Jesus has given us the instructions; now it is up to us to do more than run around in circles.

Let us pray:
O Lord, strengthen our motivation to share Christ with the world. Forgive us when we become sidetracked and treat minor issues as though they are our central purpose in life. Help us follow you and do your will on earth, as it is done in heaven. In the name of Christ, Amen.

SUGGESTED PSALM: *Psalm 138*

SUGGESTED HYMNS:

"*Rejoice, the Lord Is King*" *(B, E, F, L, P, UM, W)*

"*Rejoice, Ye Pure in Heart*" *(B, C, E, F, P, UM)*

The Promise of Power

Hearing the Word

The verses of the devotional scripture for today come from the "final discourse" of Jesus to his disciples, as recorded in John's Gospel. It is a lengthy speech that is unique to John (though similar in some ways to the speech Jesus gives shortly before his arrest and death in Matthew 24, with parallels in Mark 13 and Luke 21). Notice that the way Jesus speaks here in John is markedly different than the parable-teller of the other three Gospels. There Jesus used brief sayings and concrete, everyday illustrations to make religious points. Here Jesus seems to be talking about other-worldly matters with few, if any, references to everyday life. John's Gospel is thought to be the last of the four written, and does reflect more of the church's understanding of the triune nature of God. By the time John was written, the church was wrestling with and gaining insight about questions such as the relationship between God the Father, God the Son, and God the Holy Spirit.

Living the Word

One mother tells about a special journal she has been keeping for years. She said that she does not want to call it a diary because that would imply that she does not want anybody to read it. Instead, she has two readers in mind—her two daughters. Soon after her first daughter was born, she said, she began to wish that she could share the joys and funny stories of the things they said and did. She worried that by the time they were old enough to appreciate the stories and memories, she would not be able to remember them. Therefore she bought a bound book with blank pages and began to write to her little girls.

She is now on her second book of memories and has written more than five hundred pages an incident at a time. She said this is a way that she can always "be with them" as their mother and share the memories of their childhood with them. It is a great idea, and more parents should try it!

Some of the same feelings are written all over the page of John 16:7-14. Jesus says that he has much more to tell his disciples than they can bear to hear at this time, and yet he is hoping to get the message across to them later through the gift of the Holy Spirit. Just as this mother knew she would not always be physically present for her daughters, Jesus knew that he could not stay with his disciples, either. Yet both the mother and Jesus clearly wanted to continue to "speak," be remembered with love, and have a continuing influence.

One important difference is that the mother, no matter how much she writes in her journal, cannot anticipate every question, every need, or every situation in life for her daughters. On the other hand, through the Holy Spirit, Jesus continues to speak to us, to be alive and present for us. The guidance of the Holy Spirit is constantly available to us, given to us according to our circumstances. With God there is really a chapter on any and every subject. When we are guilty of wrongdoing, the Holy Spirit is there to confront and convict us. When we are sad and in grief, the Holy Spirit is there to comfort us. When we rejoice, the Holy Spirit is there to join in the celebration. After all, God is the one who deserves all our thanks and praise! When we are lost, the Holy Spirit is there to show us the way back "home" again. Through the Holy Spirit, Jesus is alive and present for us. Thanks be to God!

Let us pray:

Dear Creator God, we are in awe of your majestic power when we behold the mountains or ponder the stars as they march through the night. Dear Jesus, we are so thankful that you came into the world, not as a judge, but as our Savior. Dear Holy Spirit, come into our hearts like a burst of wind, and sweep away all that may stand in the way of knowing you better. In the name of Christ we pray, Amen.

Empowered by the Spirit

Hearing the Word

John 3:5-8 is a portion of the famous conversation Jesus had with Nicodemus, a Jewish official. The conversation was held at night, presumably because that is when Nicodemus could approach Jesus without the risk of being seen talking with Jesus. However, John was fond of using the symbols of darkness and light to stand for belief and lack of belief. Nicodemus was at least curious about Jesus and interested in his ideas. There is no indication in the Scriptures that he became a convert; in fact, he simply seems confused, then fades out of the story without any particular reaction. Later he comes to Jesus' defense (John 7:50-51) and helps provide a good burial for Jesus (John 19:39).

Living the Word

Let's consider three fairly typical "spiritual-birth stories."
A young couple had their first baby after being married for five years. Neither one of them had been "into church" much before they were married. However, once the baby came, a couple of their parents kept asking them when they were going to get the baby baptized. Earlier, the husband's closest friend was killed along with five other workers in a factory explosion. When he went to the funeral, a lot of what the minister said made sense to him. So when he met with the minister about the baptism, and the minister explained to him about how God would never go back on his promise to love and accept their baby, he found it very moving. Suddenly he was filled with a spiritual hunger like he had never known before. He actually wanted to go to church; he joined a Sunday school class, began to read his Bible, and gradually made several changes in his life.

A different new birth: A thirty-five-year-old man says, "I am a born-again Christian, and in Christ I am three years and four days old. Exactly three years ago this past Tuesday I gave my life to Jesus Christ at 9:35 P.M. during a tent revival meeting at the fairgrounds. I went because a friend dragged me there. I had been into drugs, booze, sleaze, bar fights; you name it, I did it. When the preacher had the altar call, I wasn't going to go up there until he told about the two friends who got hit by a train on the way home from a revival. One of them got saved that night, the other one figured he could wait to some other time. Something about that made me think about what I was doing to myself, and I went forward bawling like a baby. My friends can't believe I'm the same person, and really I'm not."

The next person, a retired woman says, "Someone asked me when I became a Christian, and I told him, 'I don't ever remember *not* being a Christian!' My parents raised me in the church; we came every Sunday, and I still do. I don't ever remember going up to an altar call or anything like that, but I've felt close to God ever since I can remember. When did it happen for me? I think it has always been happening."

Jesus told Nicodemus that we must be born not only physically, but also spiritually. After all, to live, one must first be born. Two births. Two lives (one we live, and one we might have lived). Born-again; Christian. Gradual change versus sudden change.

Our faith is meant to change our spiritual standing with God. Some Christians get hung up on one style of conversion and think that everybody must have the same kind of conversion experience they had. Thus, our new life in Christ will tend to result in changes in our thoughts, habits, values, and actions. For some people, it is a dramatic, identifiable moment in time. For others, it is a process that may last from weeks to an entire lifetime. Christ is always knocking at the door. Christ can only come into our heart when, somewhere along the way, we open the door.

Let us pray:
Dear Lord, we confess that, in some ways, we still need for you to convict and convert us. We admit that our commitment to you is too often only partial, and our new life in Christ is therefore compromised. Help us hear you knocking on the door to our heart today, and accept you with joy. Amen.

READ IN YOUR BIBLE: *1 Corinthians 1:26-31*   **March 18, 2001**
SUGGESTED PSALM: *Psalm 106:1-12*
SUGGESTED HYMNS:
  "Love Divine, All Loves Excelling" (All)
  "Amazing Grace" (All)

Empowered for Service

Hearing the Word

The Corinthian church had some problems, one of which centered around a leader by the name of Apollos, who was apparently a sophisticated, polished, highly educated individual. By contrast, Paul had been a tentmaker and not quite as sophisticated. After Paul left that church on his other travels, it was natural for some people to prefer the teachings of Apollos. This was because of his eloquence and apparent wisdom. However, it led to problems, and most of all, to the mistaken assumption that humans can, through their own wisdom, seek and find their own "salvation." With this in mind, Paul's comments in the devotional text are more easily understood. He is not saying it is good to be anti-intellectual, but he is saying that it is arrogant to think that anyone, through the pursuit of wisdom, can find God's grace. The message of God's grace appears to be foolishness to those searching for wisdom, since it would not be wise to voluntarily go to the cross. But the love and self-sacrifice it took is stronger than human wisdom.

Living the Word

I am not very wise, but at least I know it, especially after the sermon a couple of Sundays ago.

The sermon was about the disciples on the road to Emmaus who saw Jesus but didn't recognize him. To lead into it, I tried to illustrate how hard it is to remember past phone numbers when you move from place to place every few years. The morning of the sermon I quickly tried to recall some of the numbers from our past that were confusingly close.

I told the congregation that in our first three churches, our area code has switched from 309 to 217, then back to 309. To further confuse the numbers, I lived in dorm room 310 while dating, then lived in apartment 309 after marrying. Meanwhile the numbers on our street addresses have been 309 and 310 while our P.O. box numbers were 409 and 411. Then at one church we lived at 114 Salem Court, with P.O. box 413. The first three digits of the phones where we have lived have included 734, 437, and 247. When the first three numbers did not have a 7, 3, or 4 in them, the last four digits were 7040 at that location.

I listed all of these confusingly close numbers to explain why, when someone asked me my phone number recently, I accidentally gave them the area code of one church, the first three digits of a second one, and the last four digits where we live now! All this seemed to be terribly funny to the congregation. In fact, I was pleasantly surprised that they found my little aside so amusing.

It wasn't until the service was over that the rush was on to tell me that they were laughing so hard because when I tried to state my current phone number, I gave the wrong area code. In writing my notes hurriedly over breakfast, I wrote that my churches were in the 309, then 217, then 309 area codes. Really, it's exactly opposite. It should have been 217, then 309, then 217. So they were laughing, not because of me telling them how I had once been confused, but because I unintentionally proved to them, from the pulpit, how badly I was still confused.

When I have to tell my phone number now, I feel like a dizzy person wearing a blindfold. I'm thinking that after that sermon, someone will give me a button for my next birthday: "No matter what he says, this is *really* his phone number."

The point is not to put your trust, ultimately, in human wisdom, no matter how much you may like the sermon. First of all, we're really not as wise as we might think. And second, even if we could always know our own phone number, and even everything else there is to know, we are not forgiven in God's sight because of our brains. We are forgiven because of God's heart.

Let us pray:
   O Lord, thank you for your mercy and your love. Thank you for rescuing us from a life of sin and death, not because we are so smart or otherwise deserving, but because you care for us. In Jesus' name we pray, Amen.

READ IN YOUR BIBLE: *Psalm 103:15-18*   **March 25, 2001**

SUGGESTED PSALM: *Psalm 103:1-14*

SUGGESTED HYMNS:

"*There Is a Balm in Gilead*" *(B, E, F, P, UM, W)*

"*Rock of Ages, Cleft for Me*" *(B, C, E, F, L, UM)*

Spirit-Empowered Obedience

Hearing the Word

Psalm 103 is one of the most beautiful psalms in the Bible, and it has several "famous" portions. One well-known portion is today's devotional reading comparing human life to the brevity of the life cycle of grass or wildflowers. Still, the psalmist affirms that for those who honor the Lord, God's love lasts forever. The larger psalm was apparently used at least as a "thank-offering" psalm, which means that just before the community gave an offering or sacrifice to God, they might read this psalm. While today's portion contrasts the fleeting nature of life with the eternal nature of God's love, the context overall gives thanks to God for God's power, God's justice, and God's forgiveness.

Living the Word

Life can be so short! As a chaplain and minister, I can remember far too many tragic and untimely deaths, and the emotional devastation they bring to loved ones. A young boy on his tricycle, backed over in the driveway by one of his parents. A baby who died unexpectedly at birth, and the quiet pain of the parents of so many other babies miscarried before the children were even born. A teen who died in a car accident after a school dance. Another teen the victim of a drunk-driving accident. A young adult in the prime of life who collapsed and died in mid-stride at a family gathering on Christmas morning. A child killed by a gun while in the supposed safety of a friend's home. Three teens committed suicide.

In some capacity, after only fifteen years of ministry so far, I have been there with the families of all of these and of many other peo-

63

ple who have died at every age in life. One unspoken burden many ministers and other caregivers (including police, firefighters, ambulance crews, doctors, hospital personnel, and funeral directors) carry is the difficulty of sharing in such pain even in the smallest way. If you care at all for the people you serve, you cannot sleep after dealing with tragedies such as these. Yet how much harder it must have been for the families to experience such news firsthand.

Life can be brutally short. Death, like a heartless thief, comes to destroy and rob people of years of life. More than two thousand years ago, the psalmist put it this way: "As for us, our life is like grass. We grow and flourish like a wild flower; then the wind blows on it, and it is gone—no one sees it again" (Psalm 103:15-16 TEV).

All of this is depressing, of course, and could naturally lead to the question for the families: How can we go on under these circumstances? One father, when asked how he dealt with his son's death, replied, "It is not possible to bear. The pain is beyond words. You just keep breathing, and survive one unbearable hour after another. Then they stretch into weeks, and somehow you have, moment by moment, with God's help, borne the unbearable."

One thing I have noticed is that, generally speaking (and there are always exceptions), the more "untimely" the death, the more difficult it is to accept. When a teen is violently robbed of a whole future, it raises more questions than when a one-hundred-year-old dies peacefully in her sleep after a long and happy life. So one measure of the "sting" of death is how much unlived life it has stolen. The longer a person has lived, the less that death is seen as a robber and the more it can be seen as simply a transition or even a blessing.

So this psalm can be comforting. It acknowledges that life is short and often cut far too short. Yet it affirms that the Lord's love lasts forever. The power of death is to rob us of life, of joy, and of companionship. But the power of God is far greater, for in Christ we are given new life, new joy, and the constant companionship of an understanding Lord. All of these things will last throughout our life, and in God's eternal kingdom, even death cannot take them from us.

Let us pray:

Dear Lord, help us deal with the often-harsh circumstances of life, and give compassionate support to those who grieve and suffer. Help us, knowing that no day of life is ever guaranteed, live each day with love, kindness, and thankfulness. Amen.

SUGGESTED PSALM: *Psalm 5*

SUGGESTED HYMNS:

"Silent Night" *(All)*

"Hope of the World" *(E, L, P, UM, W)*

Called to Serve and Forgive

Hearing the Word

Micah 4:1-7 includes a portion that is nearly parallel to Isaiah 2:2-4. It is unusual in the Prophets, in spite of their similarities, for one to incorporate something nearly identical to a passage from another. Which of the two prophets first wrote this prophecy is relevant for better understanding. It shows, then, who incorporated it, and it makes possible a more meaningful interpretation of their editorial work of the other. At least one biblical scholar has suggested that Micah wrote it first, although Micah's book covers a much longer period of time than he could have personally lived. Chapters 4 and 5 of Micah come from a time after the Exile (which began in 586 B.C.), while chapters 1 through 3 appear to have come from a time before the Exile.

Living the Word

As of this writing, the United States has been bombing Yugoslavia about two months. The cause we are fighting for certainly seems noble and justified, yet the price is terribly high. NATO's targets include oil refineries, airplanes, bridges, buildings, tanks, anti-aircraft sites, and troop concentrations. We have already stopped their ability to produce fuel, and have blown up about half of their aircraft, cut off primary bridges and transportation routes, knocked out their key communications, and bombed hundreds of buildings. We have killed a lot of their soldiers. And, in one of the many pathetic effects of war, we have unintentionally killed innocent civilians too. For example, a bus of civilians happened to cross a bridge right when one of our planes dropped a bomb on the bridge.

Yugoslavia's side has not been innocent, however. Their soldiers have terrorized village after village, killing, raping, burning, and looting. They have either killed or forced nearly every Albanian in Kosovo to flee. Indeed, something had to be done to stop such terror and viciousness. So we are trapped, backed into a corner where violence seems to be the only answer; violence for evil, or violence for good.

So, what is the bill for the inability of Yugoslavia to live in peace with Kosovo, and NATO's consequent military action? It is difficult to estimate the amount of damage to their side in dollars, a tab our country will probably pick up when we stop bombing and then repair all the damage we've done. As for our military and refugee relief efforts, Congress has so far authorized $12 billion (that's *billion*, with a *B*). But money cannot describe the worst cost. You would have to attend the funerals of all the soldiers and civilians on both sides, and tour the businesses and homes that their side has burned or our side has bombed. You would have to live with people in their refugee camps and experience their grief and loss to tally the true cost of war. It is a terrible cost to both sides. War, even when it feels completely justified, brings no joy.

The Bible still holds out a dream, a hope that one day our weapons will become obsolete, and peace will prevail. It may seem like an impossible dream, especially with cruel leaders in the world who practice genocide and "ethnic cleansing." But this precious dream of peace must never be one we give up on. Someday, just maybe, we will find a way to spend our billions helping people build better lives instead of destroying the life they have built.

Peace is certainly the dream of anyone who has truly experienced the violence of war. Peace is the silent prayer of anyone who has clutched a screaming child in a bomb shelter after a deafening blast nearby. The wish for peace is in the tearful lament of anyone who has opened the door to be greeted by the words "I regret to inform you." Peace is surely the ardent hope of today's refugees living in tents while their homeland is being reduced to ruins.

Maybe someday there can be peace on earth. War is so sad, so costly.

Let us pray:
Lord, help us get along with each other in the world, in our nation, and in our homes. In the name of Jesus, the Prince of Peace. Amen.

SUGGESTED PSALM: *Psalm 74*

SUGGESTED HYMNS:

"*My Hope Is Built*" *(B, C, F, L, P, UM)*

"*Lift Every Voice and Sing*" *(B, E, L, P, UM, W)*

Called to Witness to All People

Hearing the Word

To the peoples of the ancient world, war was often seen as a contest between the gods of the countries who were fighting. The strongest god created victory for that country. This general idea can be seen, for example, in the colorful contest between Elijah and the prophets of Baal (see 1 Kings 18). The verses of today's devotional scripture may come from a time when Israel was facing an imminent attack by the Assyrians, and needed to be reassured that their God was stronger than the Assyrians'. Thus, even though the military power looked lopsided in favor of the other team, the Israelites could expect a miracle finish from their own leaders because of God's help.

Living the Word

I was born and raised in Decatur, Illinois, where my high school had more students than the entire population of Pleasant Hill, Illinois, the first town where I served as a minister. In my high school, unless you were at least six feet four inches or could sink 60 percent of your shots from "outside," you didn't need to try out for the basketball team. The small-town team is in a different circumstance. It can't afford to cut too many six-footers. More likely, the team will keep all of the dozen kids who try out, who represent 40 percent of the junior/senior boys in the whole school. They will probably range in size from six feet, three inches down to five feet, nothing. The team usually plays other small schools, which is fair, but they often have at least one significantly larger school on their regular schedule. Thus, at least once or twice each sporting season, we (I'm now part of the small-town crowd) must all pile in cars and buses, drive into the city, and get trounced by the big school.

It's inspiring, in a way, to watch our kids doing their best to guard their semipro basketball stars. It takes courage to try to keep a guy from shooting when you jump and wave your arms over your head but still don't interfere with his view of the basket, even if he is standing flat-footed! Maybe that is why the memory of one game is so sweet. The "routine" game, where the big school was supposed to cream us before advancing to regionals, was unexpectedly close at the half. With a second and a half left, it was our ball at half court. A pass, a shot, and the buzzer sounded, but our three-pointer swished! The pandemonium! The celebration! The tears! The joy! David beat Goliath again!

Christianity is a march of courage. So often it is waving your arms in front of the opponent whose jersey numbers are at your eye level. It is taking a stand against forces that seem impossible to defeat, forces that are all pervasive in society. Look at gambling, drugs, alcohol abuse, crime, not to mention sin itself! The list of opponents is long, and they are mostly seven-footers!

Christianity is a march of courage because we are followers of Jesus. Especially when you are the underdog, it takes raw courage to march for what you believe in. The message today is that victory is not impossible.

Today's devotional scripture reading is an attempt to give courage to the Israelites who faced the imminent invasion of the Assyrians. One did not have to be a military expert to see that the outcome was really decided before the conflict began. Assyria was the giant superpower; Israel was simply fortunate that the Assyrians had not gotten too serious about taking over. In the face of such long odds, Micah wrote to say keep believing, keep trusting in God, for God is capable of miraculous deliverance. Was he right? Well, Assyria won the battle, but look on your globe today. Can you find Israel? And what about Assyria? Keep faith. Have courage. Put your trust in God.

Let us pray:
Dear Lord, help us have the courage it takes to follow you in today's world. Amen.

Called to Proclaim the Risen Lord

Hearing the Word

John's account of Jesus' resurrection varies a bit from those of Matthew, Mark, and Luke. In John, Mary goes to the tomb alone, and no mention is made about taking spices to prepare his body for final burial. In the Synoptic Gospels, three women are the first to go to the tomb, and their purpose is clear because of the spices they are taking with them. Notice how Mary's story in John is "interrupted" by the story of Peter and "the disciple Jesus loved" (namely, John). It was important to the early church to make the point that Peter, to whom Jesus had given authority and who was their first leader, was also the first person to see Jesus and realize that he had risen. Even though Mary was the first one there, her "recognition" did not come until after the men saw Jesus and believed.

Living the Word

A church once gave me a book of clean church jokes, which I enjoyed using from time to time in the sermons. However, there were several jokes in it that I never thought were too funny. One Sunday I decided to tell one of them just as an example of how terrible some of the jokes were in the book. To my surprise, a lot of people really laughed hard at the joke! There must have been something there that I just couldn't recognize as funny.

The joke was about an elderly widow who couldn't see very well without her glasses. One day she got asked out on a date, and she was determined to impress this elderly bachelor with how young at heart she was and how much vitality she still possessed. So she planned to take him on a walk through the woods, and not wear glasses anytime on their date. Then she carefully placed a pin in the trunk of a tree. Later that evening, when they were walking through the woods, she exclaimed, "Hey, isn't that a pin stuck in that tree, up there about a hundred yards up the path? I'll go see!" So she took off running toward the tree, and tripped over a cow. (That's the end of the joke!) The only reason I tell it now is because this story, in a silly way, deals with the issue of sight and recognition. It could be an Easter parable for us all. How often do we get all wrapped up and worried about some insignificant detail (all concerned about what other people think of us) and miss the obvious that is right in front of us—we don't have to impress the Lord to gain the love of God. Further, Jesus is risen! That means we do not need to worry about all the little things. The Lord has taken care of the biggest problems that face us, such as overcoming the power of death, getting our lives right with God, and accepting us in spite of our sins.

Mary and the women were thinking about preparing Jesus' body for burial. They were so busy looking for a dead man that all of them, from Mary to the other disciples, looked Jesus right in the eye and spoke to him without recognizing him. They could see but not recognize him.

So often we feel friendless, alone, frustrated, angry, cheated, guilty, hopeless, and grieved. We may look for solutions everywhere but to God; or we may even conclude that there are no solutions. We may feel, like Mary did, that "someone must have taken my Lord away." But one of the messages of Easter is this: Even when we bow our heads in despair, the Lord is there! Like the woman in the story who needed to wear her glasses to see the cow, we need to look a little more often through the eyes of faith, so that we can see the risen Lord.

Let us pray:
O God, may our eyes be opened today, and everyday, to the presence of the risen Lord who walks with us every moment of our lives. Help us to see the Lord with us and to see everything else in its proper perspective. Through Christ, our risen Lord and constant companion. Amen.

Called to Be Inclusive

Hearing the Word

Galatians is a letter Paul wrote with great feeling and while in a difficult situation. From a distance, he had to defend not only the main points of his teaching, but also his credentials as an apostle. (It is difficult to argue on behalf of yourself about your credibility. If people do not think you are credible, it makes the argument hard to win!) The main controversy was over the question of whether male Gentile converts had to be circumcised like their Jewish counterparts. At stake was the larger question of whether salvation comes from keeping the Jewish Law, or whether it comes from faith. Paul argued that we are saved by faith alone. That is why the verses in today's devotional scripture lie at the heart of Paul's message, not only to the Galatians, but also to the world.

Living the Word

A coach told about trying to teach his young boys' beginners baseball team how to steal a base. Some of the boys were afraid to take their foot off the base, so he tried to teach them to be brave enough to take a lead-off and then to run to the next base when the pitcher threw the ball to the batter.

One little boy got on second base; the coach stood next to third base. "Now, on this next pitch, I want you to steal third base, okay?" The boy just looked nervously at the long, dirt base path, and nodded that he would try. (At that age level, there is no need to keep base-stealing a secret; if the catcher can throw the ball to the third baseman within three bounces, then there is a 95 percent chance that the ball will roll right under the third baseman's glove.)

So when the ball was pitched, the runner did not run toward third for two or three pitches, even though he promised the coach he would. Finally he ran. As the pitcher threw the ball to the batter, the runner took off toward third. The catcher threw the ball to third, and someone in the stands, probably his mother or father, screamed "Slide!" So the boy slid. Unfortunately, he was still about ten feet short of the base! True to percentages, the third baseman missed the ball, which rolled into the outfield. Instead of getting up and continuing on to the base, though, the boy just lay in the dirt on his back, his feet pointed toward third base about ten feet away. So the outfielder picked up the ball, ran over, and tagged him out as the boy lay in the dust.

The boy did just what he was told. He ran when the coach said run, and he slid when Mom or Dad told him to slide. In a way you could say he "kept the letter of the Law." But it still left him short of the base!

That's the trouble with trying to "win" in God's sight merely by keeping the letter of the Law. It always leaves us a little short of the real goal. Even if we could keep the Law to perfection, it only governs our outward conduct. What matters more is that we have faith, a saving relationship with Christ.

That little boy needed to learn the rules of baseball, but he also needed a competitive spirit, one that would make him get up out of the dust and keep striving for that next base. In the same way, the Laws have their place in our Christian life. They guide us and teach us about God's will. They also serve as a measuring stick to show us how far short we are too! But in the final analysis, the rules are not what win the game. It is the loving, forgiving spirit of God. That is where we should put our faith.

Listen to the Lord just like you would listen to a good coach. However, remember the reason we "make it home" is not because we are so good at keeping the rules, but because the Lord is so good at forgiving us when we break the rules! For when we fall short, it is the Lord who scoops us up, brushes off the dust, and carries us the rest of the way.

Let us pray:

Thank you for your love and grace. Help us put our trust in your efforts and not in our own. In the name of Jesus Christ, our merciful Savior, we pray. Amen.

READ IN YOUR BIBLE: *Ephesians 3:7-12*   **April 29, 2001**

SUGGESTED PSALM: *Psalm 46*

SUGGESTED HYMNS:

 "Lord, Whose Love Through Humble Service" (E, F, L, P, UM, W)
 "More Love to Thee, O Christ" (B, C, F, P, UM)

Reaching Out to Others

Hearing the Word

Not all great people have the privilege of knowing how great and important their work will become someday. For example, some famous artists died in poverty, but their paintings sell today for many millions of dollars each. Others enjoyed fame and luxury. The apostle Paul here certainly seems aware of his important role in the spread of Christianity, and considers himself to be privileged to be the one carrying such a vital message to the world. Yet he is humble and does not think he has done anything to justify such good fortune. The lesson scripture is linked to this scripture today because in it, Paul and Barnabas are called by the Holy Spirit to be missionaries to all people.

Living the Word

It is not uncommon on television to see a special event honoring a celebrity for all he/she has accomplished in his/her life. Besides feeling blessed and honored to receive such an outpouring of love and appreciation, most people feel humbled by the experience.

By contrast, there are those whose greatness goes unsung during their lifetime, and it is not until after their death that they are recognized. It always seems sad when a person misses out on the appreciation their talent or wisdom or skill deserves. One hopes that they at least had a healthy assessment of the importance of their own life's work, even if others did not see it at the time.

One of the people who truly changed history is the apostle Paul. What would the Christian story have been without him? It is truly amazing to get out a map of his travels. Without the benefit of modern transportation, he either walked or rode a ship all over the places marked on that map! (How long would it take you to walk three hundred miles, or twelve hundred?) Not only that, but Paul apparently wandered into a new town or city, and then struck up conversations about Jesus with perfect strangers! He continued this until he had a whole church up and running, and then moved on to another town. He didn't abandon these churches, though. He wrote letters to them and raised money for them and visited them and otherwise helped them all he could from a distance.

Paul seemed to have some self-awareness about how important his work was, but he probably could never have imagined how important it was in the scope of world history. He knew that God had called him to be a missionary to the Gentiles, and he knew that was important. If you put together all the people of your church and they have, collectively, even a tenth of Paul's sense of mission and zeal, then you have a mighty church.

Like many people who feel honored when they are being recognized for a great achievement, Paul also felt humbled. He called himself "the least of all God's people" (Ephesians 3:8 TEV), but his humbleness did not cripple his effectiveness. It was not a humbleness that prevented him from taking on large and important tasks when needed. It was a humbleness that made him recognize God's role in his success and then give credit where credit was due.

Many people have too low of an estimation of their importance in the world. "I'm just a grandmother," or "Oh, my job is simple . . . anybody could do it." But there is no such thing as "just a grandmother." To your grandchildren, you are incredibly important. Nobody else can do that job but you! You don't have to be Paul to be the one who can get the message of Christ through to a child, or share God's love and comfort with someone. Sometimes a grandparent or parent or aunt or uncle is just the right person for the job. Sometimes a Sunday school teacher or a friend or a classmate is just the right person. It is good to know how important we are to God and to God's work in the world. God can use us all and needs us all for God's work.

Let us pray:

Dear Lord, open my eyes to the opportunities around me to be at work for you. Use me to share the love and salvation of Jesus Christ. Help me appreciate how important that work is and humbly accept each gentle calling as it comes. In the name of Christ, who also came as a servant of others. Amen.

SUGGESTED PSALM: *Psalm 47*
SUGGESTED HYMNS:

   "*Guide Me, O Thou Great Jehovah*" (B, C, E, F, P, UM)
   "*God, Who Stretched the Spangled Heavens*" (B, E, L, P, UM, W)

Opening New Doors

Hearing the Word

There are several psalms that fall into a special category called "enthronement psalms." They are Psalms 29, 47, 93, 95, 96, 97, 98, and 99. They were used, probably during or after a religious procession carrying the ark of the covenant, during the New Year festival. The purpose of the psalms is to affirm God's enthronement as the king of the Israelites. Remember that for a time in their history the Jewish people rejected having earthly kings; instead, they affirmed that their only king was God. For earthly rulers they had "judges." Eventually they had leaders called "kings" (Saul was the first, then David, Solomon, and others), although they still celebrated the Lord's sovereignty over not just their country, but all other nations and over all of creation.

Living the Word

Consider a fictional scene from a wedding rehearsal (one that will take many ministers back to that time when they figured out that theology class didn't really prepare them to run a smooth wedding rehearsal).

The minister arrived about fifteen minutes early for a 5:30 rehearsal on Friday evening, as planned. He was surprised that most of the people were there already. "This was supposed to begin at 5:30, wasn't it?" he asked.

The florist spoke up. "Yes, I'm sorry I forgot to call you. I asked the bride and groom to change the time to 5:00 because I have dinner plans at 6:00. But that's all right. I got a key from the janitor, and we've already started."

Without taking a breath, she continued, "Here, Reverend, I think instead of standing up on the step, you should stand facing the other way, so that the congregation can see the couple's faces."

"Thank you for that suggestion," he replied, "but I thought I would—"

At that the bride interrupted. "Mom, where do you think we should stand?"

The mother replied, "Why don't you say the vows over there, facing each other, and then the minister could step aside while you go up there for the unity candle."

The florist said, "But what would she do with her bouquet up there?"

And so it goes. Finally, as the florist and the bride's aunt locked horns on whether the groomsmen should do the halting "stutter" step with the bridesmaids, the bride looked helplessly at the minister for help in settling the matter. "Who's in charge of that part, anyway?" she asked. At that moment the minister remembered the bishop's hand on his head at the ordination service, and heard the words "Take thou authority."

There are some times in life when we all feel out of control. You hit a patch of ice on an overpass and suddenly you are looking out the windshield and seeing where you have been. You move to a new community a block away from the grade school so that your kids can walk, and the very next year the school board decides to consolidate and bus your kids fifteen miles away. A doctor says the word "cancer." A child drives a car for the first time. Who is in charge in the world? Who can we turn to that will be responsible for making everything right?

This psalm makes a bold statement: God is in charge, the king of all creation. We may not understand the whole story, but the storyteller is still God. We may not always be in control, and we may wonder at times, especially in the middle of a scary story, Who's in charge, anyway? The answer is simple to say, yet most difficult at times to live with. The rest of the story has yet to be told, but God is the one who is in charge of giving it a beautiful ending.

Let us pray:
Lord, help us have the confidence to acknowledge that you are in charge. In the midst of all of our legitimate questions and fears and doubts, draw near to help us. Increase our sense of peace and faith in you. Amen.

READ IN YOUR BIBLE: *Romans 3:21-26*   **May 13, 2001**

SUGGESTED PSALM: *Psalm 51:1-10*

SUGGESTED HYMNS:

  "Just As I Am, Without One Plea" (B, C, E, F, P, UM)

  "Holy, Holy, Holy" (All)

Defending the Truth

Hearing the Word

Romans 3:21 says, "But now God's way of putting people right with himself *has been revealed*" (TEV italics added). The idea of "revelation" is an important theological principle, and helps us understand Paul's thought. Science learns about an object or animal or ecosystem by doing study or research. This is human investigation, and implies that an object is waiting to be discovered. God, on the other hand, is a mystery. No amount of study can reveal anything that God does not want us to know. Jesus was an important way that God voluntarily revealed himself to humanity, for in Jesus' life and teachings we learned about God's will for us and about God's nature. This enables Paul to throw out the Old Testament system of being put right with God by keeping God's laws. Instead, because of God's revelation in Jesus' teaching, life, and death, we now know that God puts us right through our faith in Christ.

Living the Word

As the weather got warmer, the pool opened for the first time of the season. New management had taken over the traditional summer spot, and a new sign greeted the youthful guests on opening day. In bold red letters, it proclaimed, "Girls and boys with long hair must wear swimming caps in the pool area at all times."

The new rule angered a young man who had long flowing hair. He felt that wearing a plastic swim cap would compromise his style with the girls. So he confronted the pool's new owner. "Hey," he said, "what's with this new rule? Boys shouldn't have to wear caps. Those are just for girls."

The new owner was unmoved. "No, they are for people with long hair, and you, son, have long hair."

"But," protested the young man, "the other owners didn't make us wear swim caps."

The new owner replied, "True, but then again, they aren't the ones making up the rules anymore."

Remembering that the owner went to church, the youth decided to try a religious approach. "You know," he said, "long hair isn't so bad. Jesus and Moses had long hair."

"That's right," agreed the owner. "If they come here, they are welcome to part the water, walk on it, or even change it to wine. But if they want to swim, they'll have to put on a cap too."

Sometimes the rules change. We get a notice from the bank, and guess what—the free checking account is still free, as long as you maintain an average daily balance of $2,000 or more. But if the balance drops below that, you will be charged a $3 fee for the month! What was once free is now something you must earn.

The rules have changed with God too, but with God, the rules have changed in the opposite way. What we once had to earn is now free. Once we had to "earn" our good graces with God through keeping the Law. But that did not work in practice. As Paul points out, "everyone has sinned and is far away from God's saving presence" (Romans 3:23 TEV). So instead, God has revealed a new plan for our eternal "checking account." Instead of us running in the red all the time, now Jesus has paid our debt for us and closed the account against further debt.

While we once had to measure ourselves against the Law and never compared favorably, now we are able to focus our efforts on honoring God with our gifts of faithfulness and obedience. Obligation has become a gift. Joy is restored to living. Our failure has become God's success. We are restored in God's grace.

A bumper sticker, in its simple way, summed up the point: "Christians aren't perfect, just forgiven."

Let us pray:
We thank you, Lord, that you have come into the world through Jesus Christ, not to be our judge, but to be what we really needed most—our Savior. Amen.

READ IN YOUR BIBLE: *Philippians 1:3-11*   **May 20, 2001**
SUGGESTED PSALM: *Psalm 131*
SUGGESTED HYMNS:
  "Morning Has Broken" (B, E, F, P, UM, W)
  "My Faith Looks Up to Thee" (B, C, E, F, L, P, UM)

Responding to Need

Hearing the Word

Although the words of Philippians 1:3-11 are full of kindness and graciousness, behind the scenes the picture is not so pretty. Paul is writing this letter from prison to the first church he established in modern-day Europe (see v. 7). Not only were things not going well for Paul, but there was trouble back at this early church too. There were false teachers there, and some people were opposed to Paul. His supporters had sent a gift to help him, so one of the reasons he wrote was to thank them for the gift. But his real concern was to help people learn to discern between truth and false teaching. In the letter he seemed confident that they would do it, and he tried to encourage them in spite of his own personal hardships.

Living the Word

A couple were celebrating their fiftieth anniversary. When asked how they stayed together so long, the man said, "The secret is right here on my watch. When we got married, Mary Lou's father gave me this watch. He had these words engraved on the glass, so that I would see them every time I wanted to know what time it was. The words are, 'Say something nice to Mary Lou.' "

That seems like simple advice, but it is also powerful. When everything is going great, it is pretty easy to say something nice. But there are certainly many times in a marriage when it is tempting to say words that hurt the relationship, or use a tone of voice that does not sound like there is even an ounce of affection or friendship! Maybe we all—whether we are married or single—need a watch like that with the words, "Say something nice to someone you love."

There are some people you can meet on the street—perfect

strangers—and the one comment they will have for you is, "This sure is lousy weather, isn't it?" or "Did you ever see a postal clerk that was as slow as he is?" Other people are more like the sunshine than the rain. Paul seems like he may have been like that. If he had not mentioned being in prison just briefly, then you would never know it from these verses. They are full of kindness and gratitude. That must not have been easy, especially because he was also concerned about problems in the church.

Sometimes a parent will tell a whining child, "If you can't say anything nice, don't say anything at all." Most of us could think of things to complain about; it is much more noble and pleasant to think of kind things to say, though.

Optimist International has a creed that its members repeat at each meeting. It reminds me of Paul's disposition and is worth reading often. Here it is:

Promise Yourself—to be so strong that nothing can disturb your peace of mind. To talk health, happiness, and prosperity to every person you meet. To make all your friends feel that there is something in them. To look at the sunny side of everything and make your optimism comes true. To think only of the best, to work only for the best, and to expect only the best. To be just as enthusiastic about the success of others as you are about your own. To forget the mistakes of the past and press on to the greater achievements of the future. To wear a cheerful countenance at all times and give every living creature you meet a smile. To give so much time to the improvement of yourself that you have no time to criticize others. To be too large for worry, too noble for anger, too strong for fear, and too happy to permit the presence of trouble.

This creed may not be printed in the Bible, but Paul certainly modeled it in what he wrote. And the world would be a better place if more Christian people could put their faith into actions such as those described in this creed. All we have to do is remember that with the Lord, the news is always good, the day is always brighter than it would be without the Lord, and the future with God is certain to be good.

Let us pray:
Dear Lord, change my discouraging words into shared joy. Change my gossip into compliments. Change my complaints into praise. Change my "half-empty" dispositions into a grateful "half-full" outlook. Sanctify my thoughts and words and attitudes with your presence, which spreads light, love, joy, and peace. In Jesus' name, Amen.

Serving with Faith and Confidence

Hearing the Word

These verses are important for several reasons. First, they are another source besides the Gospel accounts of the Resurrection appearances, and they help show how the early church interpreted the Resurrection. The reference of Jesus appearing to more than five hundred believers could be something unrecorded in the Gospels, though at least one scholar suggested that it could be some kind of reference to the day of Pentecost. Even though that was the coming of the Holy Spirit instead of an appearance of the resurrected Christ, Paul said, "last of all, he appeared also to me," even though we might attribute his conversion experience to the Holy Spirit, since it was after the ascension of Jesus. In any case, these packed verses also give us a glimpse of the guilt Paul felt about persecuting the church, and by implication they indicate a pejorative term that Paul's critics might have applied to Paul ("someone whose birth was abnormal"). Since he was not one of the original disciples but still took on such a key leadership role, some may have thought he was overstepping his boundaries or speaking without the same authority from Christ.

Living the Word

A newspaper article told about a woman who died tragically and needlessly in a car accident. She drove out in front of an oncoming truck because someone had taken down the stop sign at that intersection. Soon the news broke that the missing sign was found.

81

Several teens had been out stealing traffic signs. Naturally, the wrath of a whole community came down on those kids. They were responsible for the death of the loving mother of young children.

How would a person ever recover from a "sin" like that one?

Probably the best advice would be for the boys to make a sincere apology to anyone and everyone, and then to redouble their efforts to make their own lives productive and good. After all, the family left behind would probably get no real or lasting satisfaction out of seeing any more lives destroyed. As difficult as it would be, the thing to do would be to go living much humbler and wiser, much more determined to "redeem" the gift of life.

Paul had to struggle with a similar issue. He participated in the killing of Stephen, the first Christian martyr. As he was dying, just like Jesus did, Stephen said "Lord, do not remember this sin against them". After that, Paul went on to drag Christians out of their homes and have them thrown into jail. He was out to destroy the church. Later when he was trying to build up the church, that memory haunted him. You can feel his guilt in today's passage when he says, "I do not even deserve to be called an apostle, because I persecuted God's church" (v. 9). He goes on to say, "But by God's grace I am what I am, and the grace that he gave me was not without effect" (v. 10). In other words, Paul made the most of God's second chance.

That attitude makes Paul a great model for us all. Most people have something in their past that is embarrassing or shameful or maybe even criminal, whether or not they were caught. We may know that God has forgiven us, and maybe we have even forgiven ourselves. But we still remember, and the memory is painful. Like Paul, we all have those "ghosts of sins past." But a life spent beating up on ourself is not God's way of handling sin, is it? When God forgives us, it is meant to give us the freedom to learn from our mistakes and then to go on with an even better life.

Do we truly believe in God's mercy and new life? Can we accept it for ourselves? Can we offer it to others and be sure it does not go "without effect," even for those who may feel their lives are completely destroyed by their deeds? God will help!

Let us pray:

Lord, have mercy upon us. Please do not let your mercy be wasted on us; help us to change, grow, and embrace the new life you offer in Christ. Amen.

Choose Wisely

Hearing the Word

The first part of this short section sounds a lot like something from John's Gospel; it is heavy on relationships between persons in the Trinity and light on practical, down-to-earth teachings. However, it helps set the stage for what is to follow. The second part, however, are beautiful words that have helped many people through the centuries. As is more typical of the Synoptic Gospels, Jesus uses an image from the everyday world of farming. A yoke is a harness for an animal of labor, designed to fit over the neck or shoulders. When the animal must pull a wagon or tool, the yoke gives the animal support for a heavy load. Just as a farmer puts the yoke on a new farm animal that has tired out, in the same way Jesus promises to help us with our loads when they become too heavy.

Living the Word

A tall office building under construction in a large city was to be covered with large, thin slabs of white marble. All over the ground around the building were piles of marble pieces, each one at least five feet wide by ten feet long. In order to place the slabs on the building, they had to be hoisted by a crane into place. First the crane would be positioned above a pile of marble. Then a workman on the ground would hook several cables around the rectangle to keep it from slipping out. When it was ready, he would give a "thumbs up" sign to the crane operator, who would then lift the piece of marble off the stack. Once the slab was positioned near the building, several workers would guide the piece into position and attach it. Of course, while they guided the heavy stone high up in the air, the real weight of it was borne by the crane towering above their heads.

This scene is a parable of how life with Christ can be. There are many heavy burdens that we bear in life. Christ is like the crane from above, the quiet strength that helps us lift the burdens of life.

Sometimes our burdens are stacked one on top of another; like those of a person who loses two or more loved ones in a short period of time, or of someone who has a car wreck, loses a job, loses a family member, and loses good health all in the same month. Other burdens are so difficult and challenging by themselves that it takes only one to leave us as helpless as a single worker standing next to a tall pile of rock slabs. Human strength cannot budge them; likewise, some burdens are simply impossible to bear alone. The only way we can endure them at all is by sharing them with friends, with family, and with the Lord.

There is an old saying: "A shared burden is half a burden. A shared joy is twice the joy." While this seems illogical, experience bears it out. There is something cathartic and healing about sharing a burden with another person. Even though talking about a problem does not seem to change the circumstances, it can still make us feel like a weight has been lifted from our shoulders. It can also be a great source of comfort and help to share our deepest pain and burdens with the Lord, who, even more than a friend, understands us perfectly and whose love for us will never end.

Some people do not talk about their problems, saying that sharing our burdens does not change the circumstances. On the contrary, it does. If the worker who stood next to the pile of marble had come to work alone, then he may as well have turned around and gone back home. There would be no way for him to carry even one of those pieces and place it on the building. But the presence of others changed the circumstance, and made the lifting of the burden possible. In the same way, the fact that others around us are concerned and are praying with us is a different circumstance than struggling through a problem in isolation. There is something encouraging in knowing we are supported by the love of family, friends, church, and the Lord. Jesus is our loving friend who has come to help us bear the impossible and to multiply the joy of life.

Let us pray:
Lord, thank you for your help when we are aware of it, and for your unseen hand that sustains and lifts and encourages us throughout each day. Amen.

SUGGESTED PSALM: *Psalm 17*

SUGGESTED HYMNS:

"*A Mighty Fortress Is Our God*" *(All)*

"*Guide Me, O Thou Great Jehovah*" *(B, C, E, F, P, UM)*

Follow Instructions

Hearing the Word

Most of the book of Job is a conversation between Job, who represents one point of view, and his three friends, who represent another. Elihu (the name means "He [God] is my God"), who has a single six-chapter-long speech in the book, is speaking in this section. At this point in the overall conversation, Job's friends have given up trying to convince Job of his error, and Job has issued a final challenge to God. God answers Job and his friends at the end of the book; but in between Job's final challenge and God's reply is this speech of Elihu, who claims great personal wisdom (see Job 36:3-4, for example) and who argues on God's behalf.

Living the Word

I will always remember one of the first patients I met when I was in training as a hospital chaplain. This particular young man had his arms, legs, and body wrapped in various casts and bandages. He probably had a hundred stitches all across his face, and terrible swelling and bruising. He looked like he had been hit by a train, and in fact, he had. It had rolled his car in front of it for several hundred feet before pushing the car down an embankment. It was a miracle the man survived. It turned out he had been drinking, and on a lark he tried to beat the train across the track. That was just one of his multiple problems. He had gotten into drugs; his wife had left him for mistreating her; he had lost his job; and his life had been going downhill fast. In spite of his injuries, he seemed happy and peaceful. He said that, to him, the train wreck was God's wake-up call. God was telling him to shape up, and the train certainly got his attention.

As a chaplain, I did a lot of listening, but inside I often wanted to ask, Does God really clobber people with trains because they need to "shape up"? This is the basic question the book of Job wrestles with. When bad things happen to people, what is God's role in the bad event? Is it punishment for doing something wrong? Or do bad things happen for a myriad of other reasons, making God's role more like the rescue workers who start with a bad situation and try to bring about recovery. Now that I have spent time talking with that man and others whose life stories are woven into Job, I think the latter is true. What do you think?

If we say that God's role was to make that accident happen, then we have a problem, given our admittedly limited human understanding of justice. That man abused drugs and alcohol, but does that deserve a train wreck? What should gossip get? or adultery? Why do some sinners live on and on, while some seemingly innocent and wonderful people suffer and die young? Both Job and the book of Ecclesiastes question the justice of any earthly idea of a reward and punishment system. And that is not compatible with our belief that God is just, treating all the same.

So why did the accident happen? Well, one reason is that it was a bad idea to race the train, and if he had been driving under the influence, that might contribute to the explanation too. Other train accidents happen due to faulty crossings, or bad weather, or a host of other reasons; but is God to blame for those accidents? I think not; it is difficult to imagine a loving God delivering that much earthly pain and suffering for any sin.

That does not mean that God is distant and uninvolved. Surely God was at work in the rescue efforts, in the people who brought compassion and help to the family and the victim, and in the skill of the medical team and others helping. As every stitch comes out and every bone mends, leaving behind a newly useful body, God can be seen at work. And if sitting around in so many casts sparked the thought that God wanted this person to change his life, then surely God fans the flames for such healthy thoughts.

Let us pray:
O Lord, in the midst of the mysteries and challenges that suffering presents, help us notice your healing hand at work. Help us see and thank you for all the good things you bring into our life, including the good that you can still recreate even after the worst of life's situations. Amen.

READ IN YOUR BIBLE: *Joshua 24:14-18*   **June 17, 2001**

SUGGESTED PSALM: *Psalm 125*

SUGGESTED HYMNS:

"*Stand Up, Stand Up for Jesus*" (B, C, E, F, L, UM)

"*Holy God, We Praise Thy Name*" (E, F, L, P, UM, W)

Remain Committed

Hearing the Word

Near the end of his life, Moses gave a long farewell speech to the Israelites. In it, he reminded the Israelites of all they had been through, how good God had been to them, and he asked them to recommit themselves to the Lord. Joshua, who took over after Moses, also had a long career leading the Israelites. Instead of leading them through the wilderness, as Moses had, Joshua led them into the promised land. Like Moses, here Joshua gives a farewell speech near the end of his life. In it he reminds the people of God's faithfulness to them, and urges the people to remain faithful to God. These famous words, often found printed on modern-day religious merchandise, ask the people to make a commitment. As a true leader would, Joshua inspires the people to follow by boldly taking a stand for God.

Living the Word

Marriage is a choice, a promise made to one person that involves forsaking all other potential mates. Our romanticized version of marriage is "I'll stay with you (as long as I find you the most attractive person I know)." But sooner or later someone more attractive comes along, and we have to deal with that fact. It could be that the "new" person finds you incredibly attractive too. Meanwhile, the home scene is predictable and maybe even dull. The husband is fat and bald, and burps at the dinner table. But the coworker is smart and handsome and rich and funny. He always wears a snazzy suit and leaves thoughtful gifts on your desk. You've never heard him burp at business dinners.

In short, he is more attractive. What are you going to do about

87

it? That is the moment of choice. Marriage is intended to be a life-long choice even when other options glitter more brightly. Remember, "I take thee . . . and forsake all others."

Sometimes we can't understand why the people in the Bible were attracted to idols; shouldn't it have been a simple choice between a stone/metal idol and our living God? What was the attraction to idols? Idols are things that we put in God's rightful place. Whatever we put at the center of our life, whatever motivates us to get up in the morning, whatever preoccupies our minds—those are our gods. Are you thinking, How can I make more money next year? Why doesn't this person pay me back? I can't volunteer to help poor kids read; think of all the money I would lose by volunteering." It's all a choice. The money may glitter like a romantic invitation to a burpless dinner, but Jesus said you can't serve both God and money. Make a choice. Choose this day whom you will serve.

Why choose "this day?" To put off a decision like that is really to decide no. "I'm going to lose weight and start exercising . . . tomorrow." But today is the only day you really get to decide anything. Why choose "this day"? Because the things we really care about we will make time to do sooner rather than later. Why choose "this day"? Because it is meaningless to say that we will hold a different value tomorrow if we reject it today. It is like a robber saying, "I agree that I should quit robbing, so after I rob one more bank, I'll quit my criminal ways." It is like a child, gawking at a television set, saying "Okay, Mom, I'm coming to eat right now" after being beckoned to come to dinner again and again. Finally, the mother says, "If you are going to eat, turn that thing off now!" Sooner or later the real decision has to be made.

So when you close this book, it is time once again to make up your mind. Our heavenly Parent is calling us into the world to serve God and our neighbor. God is calling us to stop staring at the glamour and glitter of money and every other thing that immobilizes our Christian walk, and to come be with the Lord's family.

Today, right now, this minute! The time to make our decision about God has come.

Let us pray:
Lord, forgive us for saying yes with our mouth and no with our life. May our commitment to you be solid as a rock, just as yours is to us, that we may experience the love and joy of being part of your family feast. Amen.

SUGGESTED HYMNS:

"*Lift Every Voice and Sing*" (B, E, L, P, UM, W)

"*Lord, I Want to Be a Christian*" (B, C, F, P, UM, W)

Speak Truth

Hearing the Word

Most of the individual proverbs in the section given in today's devotional reading have something to do with the spoken word. Several of them deal with the issue of truth-telling versus lying, and the integrity of what we say. In the lesson scripture, the prophet Micaiah was faced with the difficult prospect of telling the unpopular truth. The other prophets bailed out on their responsibility and told King Ahab what he wanted to hear, and at first Micaiah did too. But then the king scolded him for not saying what he really thought! A lie doesn't do anyone a favor in the long run.

Living the Word

Several boys were standing around a puppy on a street corner. A minister walked by and was curious when he heard one of the boys say, "Then they let my parents off the UFO out behind the garden, and ever since then they have been acting strange." The preacher stopped and pretended to read a poster nearby, so that he could listen. "Oh, that's nothing," said another boy. "My dad fell in a pit in the backyard that was full of thousands of rattlesnakes, and he didn't even get bit."

At that the minister could take it no longer. He walked up to the boys and asked, "What are you boys doing? What's all this about UFOs and rattlesnakes?"

One of the boys from his church looked a little sheepish. "Well," he admitted, "we just found this puppy here, and we all wanted him. So we decided whoever could tell the biggest lie would get to take the puppy home."

"My gosh, boys!" admonished the cleric. "I've never heard of such a thing! Why, when I was a boy, I would never have even dreamed of telling lies!"

At that the boys looked at each other dejectedly. "Well," said one finally, "I guess the Reverend wins the dog."

The book of Proverbs is a collection of wise sayings. They are meant to instruct people on how to live a righteous life. One of the most common themes in Proverbs has to do with our words. That may be because our words are one of the most difficult things to control, and also because words have incredible power either to hurt or to help.

Think how easily a stellar reputation built up for an entire life-time can be undone in a listener's mind with words like these: "I heard she had an affair with Mr. Smith," or "If you want to trust him with your money, go ahead. Just don't come crying to me when it mysteriously disappears." When passing along anything negative about any other person, even a comment like "She always acts cold to me," an angel wearing black-and-white referee stripes should burst on the scene shouting, "Technical foul! Time out! Other side is awarded several free shots!"

Words are also our canvas for painting misleading pictures. Lies. Half-truths. Knowing omissions that lead to the wrong impression. Harmful implications. Damaging innuendos. We must live in such a way that we are not ashamed of the truth—the exact and complete truth. Since we cannot be perfect, we need to be humble, and willing to let the exact truth humble us when it is tempting to lie and cover for ourselves. Humbleness is a powerful teacher and motivator. Proverbs says, "A lie has a short life, but truth lives on forever" (Proverbs 12:19 TEV).

Proverbs says, "Thoughtless words can wound as deeply as any sword, but wisely spoken words can heal" (Proverbs 12:18 TEV). A good resolution for everybody: Read Proverbs more, talk less. And when you talk, let it be words that are both true and words that build others up.

Let us pray:

Lord, just as a wild horse is brought under control by a bit in its mouth, help us bring the power of our words under your control, that you may use everything we say for your purposes and glory. In Jesus' name, Amen.

READ IN YOUR BIBLE: *Hebrews 10:26-30*　　　　**July 1, 2001**
SUGGESTED PSALM: *Psalm 75*
SUGGESTED HYMNS:
"*America*" *(B, E, F, L, P, UM, W)*
"*America the Beautiful*" *(B, C, E, F, P, UM, W)*

Consequences of Disobedience

Hearing the Word

In the Old Testament system of laws and sacrifices, making a sacrifice covered sins committed unintentionally. However, if someone deliberately sinned, thinking, "Oh, I can just kill an animal later and that will pardon me," then that sacrifice was hollow and ineffective. In fact, under the old law, that person deserved to die for knowingly disregarding God's Laws.

Here Paul, or whoever wrote Hebrews (scholars debate whether Paul did or someone else), makes an analogy; if relying on the sacrifice of an animal to cover deliberate sins deserved death under the old system, then think how much more serious it is to take the sacrifice of Jesus lightly and to see it as a license to sin.

Living the Word

Two proverbs come to mind after reading this scripture. The first one: "A wise person will try to keep the king happy; if the king becomes angry, someone may die" (Proverbs 16:14 TEV). It is wise to acknowledge that there are those who have some kind of power over us, and to respect them and their power. Not to do so is folly.

For example, the recent real-life police TV shows allow the average person to come along and observe human behavior at its worst. Perpetrators spit at police officers, swear at them, threaten to sue them, run from them, crash into their cars, and even swing at them. They have no respect for the law, or even for the simple fact that they are starting a fight with someone who is an armed and skilled marksman! This is a study for folly personified. What is most impressive and amazing is the level of courtesy, patience, and professionalism the officers show these people.

Likewise, we believe that God is full of grace and mercy, and that is right. But it is still not wise to forget who God is, nor the incredible power that God has. Just because we talk about God's love and mercy is no reason to assume that God is a weak powder puff. This part of Hebrews wisely reminds us to remember God's awesome potential if our actions make God into our enemy.

The second Proverb amplifies a different point found here in Hebrews: "Don't hesitate to discipline children. A good spanking won't kill them. As a matter of fact, it may save their lives" (Proverbs 23:13-14 TEV).

God's judgment is not intended to be abusive or violent. Rather, it serves as a motivator to get us moving in the right direction. Consider an example. Some dogs bark incessantly. You can stick your head out the door and ask nicely, "Please don't bark." But after the dog has finished laughing at you, it goes right back to barking! That's where a barking collar comes in handy. You just put it around the dog's neck, and the dog quickly learns that when it barks, the collar delivers an unpleasant shock. From then on, you usually don't have to put that collar on the dog. You can simply lay it where the dog can see it, and that usually inspires cooperation.

God is full of grace and love, but that doesn't mean God will ignore disrespect, or allow his love to be trampled. Just before today's passage, the writer positively appeals to readers to do God's will. That works with most people most of the time. God is willing to do everything possible to get us moving in the right direction. So in today's scripture the writer does not exactly deliver a shock, but he does lay down the shock collar in full view where we can see it and consider whether we really want to disobey Almighty God.

Let us pray:
O Lord, keep us moving in the right direction! Thank you for your love and kindness. Help us remember that your power, so fearful if we stand against you, is the same power working for us when we choose to remain in fellowship with you. Amen.

SUGGESTED PSALM: *Psalm 107:1-9, 43*
SUGGESTED HYMNS:
 "Be Thou My Vision" (B, E, F, P, UM)
 "How Firm a Foundation" (All)

Empty Offerings

Hearing the Word

Malachi, one of the twelve "minor" prophets, is the last book of the Old Testament. It comes from the last period in Israel's history covered by the "history" books of the Old Testament, Ezra and Nehemiah. They record a time following the Babylonian exile, when the Israelites had the opportunity to return to the promised land and rebuild the temple. This prophet spoke to the people sometime after that, when the people had grown lax in their faith. In today's reading, Malachi attacks the priests and the offerings the people bring as evidence of how low of a priority God is to them.

Living the Word

I had the opportunity to work in the warehouse for UMCOR (United Methodist Committee on Relief), located in Baldwin, Louisiana. All the workers are volunteers from around the country who come to help receive, sort, and ship relief supplies domestically and internationally to people in disaster areas. One of the professional staff persons there gave our group a tour. We looked at huge piles of boxes that come into the warehouse by way of mail, UPS, personal vehicles, and semitrailers. Some boxes were filled with expensive medications, others with baby or school or health supplies. As we prepared to tackle the pile of boxes, the staff stressed a point over and over to us: "The people who receive these gifts are regular people, just like you and me, who have been through a flood or hurricane or other disaster. So when you sort through these items, think about how you would feel if you received it. If you would use it gladly, then let it pass through. If you would not want to wear it or use it, then let's either wash it or fix it or find some other use for it."

Most of the donated items were brand new or in great shape. But some weren't. As an example, she showed us cloth diapers sent for relief supplies. Unfortunately, they were badly stained. Would you want to put those on your baby? Some of the blouses were torn or missing buttons down the front. Some of the shoes were caked with mud or simply worn out, and so on. The point she made was that if we were going to pass along a gift to someone, we wanted to be sure to show real respect for them as people. The warehouse was not meant to be used so people could "clean out their closets"—the stuff they don't want either. A real gift is something of value, not something you couldn't bring yourself to throw away.

In the same way, Malachi tells the Israelites that they were wrong to slight God by picking out the undesirable animals in their herd to sacrifice. It is an insult to God to offer just the things the people themselves did not really want. Instead, the Almighty God deserves our best.

This raises questions for us, not only in our giving habits, but also in our living habits. First, consider how you decide what to give to God's service. Are the gifts you offer something that you would, if you kept it, really consider important? Or is the ten-dollar bill ceremoniously pitched into the plate each week "just a slice off the fat of the land" for you—something of no real consequence? Do you plan how much to give, and what factors do you consider? Have you ever given away something that you truly treasure, and know that it will therefore mean a great deal to the recipient? It is a good idea to reconsider our giving habits.

This dramatic call in Malachi should also give us an incentive to consider our living habits. In your average day, what time does God get? Can you make a slice of prime morning time to give God, or, if you do a devotional reading, is it always relegated to the time of day you are either distracted or exhausted? It is better to make some time than no time, of course! But still, when we carefully put certain appointments in our calendar book like they are made of gold, and crowd out even a spare moment to have a religious thought, doesn't that say something about us that we need to reconsider?

Let us pray:

Dear Lord, forgive us when we equate giving with getting rid of things we don't want. Teach us to be generous enough to share meaningful gifts that honor the recipient, and especially you. In Jesus' name, who gave his life. Amen.

SUGGESTED PSALM: *Psalm 95:1-7*
SUGGESTED HYMNS:
 "Rejoice, the Lord Is King" (B, E, F, L, P, UM, W)
 "Rejoice, Ye Pure in Heart" (B, C, E, F, P, UM)

Broken Vows

Hearing the Word

Psalm 100 was originally created as a psalm for a thank offering. The setting might have been the act of taking an offering to the Temple, and this psalm might have been used as a call to worship, or perhaps as a procession approached the Temple. It can be broken down into four "stanzas." The first, verses 1-2, call the worshiper to sing and worship with joy. The second, verse 3, is what links this with today's lesson scripture, because it reminds the reader of the covenantal relationship with God, which is a theme (or the lack of such a relationship) in Hosea. The third, verse 4, calls the worshiper to enter with praise and thanksgiving, and the last stanza could be a response to the third, as it contains just such words of "praise."

Living the Word

A youth group from our church went to a concert of a well-known Christian music artist. As the pastor of our small rural church and the leader of the youth group, I sat with them high up in a huge stadium, our voices swallowed up in a sea of twenty thousand excited young people. Suddenly the lights dimmed. After a tremendous fanfare of clashing cymbals, blaring music, and an impressive display of laser lights, the musician suddenly burst from a cloud of blue fog on the stage. The roar from the crowd was deafening. He shouted in the microphone, "Everybody, give Jesus a hand!" So everyone applauded for Jesus. Then, like a cheerleader at a high school basketball game, he had the crowd on their feet screaming Jesus' name as loud as they could—one side of the stadium competing against the other to show the most enthusiasm. Even kids from my own youth group, who have been told to "sit down and be quiet" since they were two years old, were standing up and shouting.

Then this singer had his keyboard player do a parody of "church." He played an old hymn, making the notes tremble sadly like funeral-home music. "That's not church!" the singer suddenly screamed, interjecting the jab at many mainline churches. "Who wants to go to a church like that?" he questioned rhetorically. The standing youth gave the "thumbs down" gesture and booed.

I took his shot at traditional mainline worship services to heart. Frankly, it had enough truth in it to hurt. We had all been to church that very morning, and the music sounded a little like his keyboard player had presented it. But could we help it that the one instrument the church had was a thirty-year-old electronic organ that happens to sound just like the same kind of organ over at the funeral home? And if I shouted, "What have you come here to do?" at my congregation, three-fourths of whom are way past retirement age, they would certainly not leap up from their pews and scream "Praise the Lord!" Some of them would turn down their hearing aids if I shouted at them, but they would not dance around. So, does that make them wrong to want a worship service without screaming and dancing in it?

Psalm 100 bids us to come into God's presence with joy, happy songs, and thanksgiving. There are too many people who drag in expecting to be bored at church. Too many people think it is a sin to smile at a joke or clap for the kids in the sanctuary. Of course worship should have some time for quiet, reflective prayer. But this psalm is a reminder that joy and celebration is healthy too.

Even if your church does not have a laser light show and a rock band, worship should not depend on the "entertainment" up front. Worship is really in our hearts. No matter where we go, we can and should bring whatever joy we have with us, and truly be thankful for all of God's gifts. Jesus came to forgive, to be a friend, and to show how much God loves us. Count your blessings, be happy, and celebrate!

Let us pray:
O Lord, open our mouths, so that we may speak and sing your praises. Open our hearts, that we might receive you and worship you with joy. Amen.

SUGGESTED PSALM: *Psalm 100*
SUGGESTED HYMNS:
  "Amazing Grace" (All)
  "Jesus, Lover of My Soul" (B, C, E, F, P, UM)

Rejected Love

Hearing the Word

Like Psalm 100 from last week's devotional reading, this psalm was originally created to be used to present a thank offering at the Temple. It celebrates the love and goodness of God, comparing God's care to that of a parent for a child. God's anger and judgment against sin is not pushed aside, but the love of God puts that anger in perspective. God's anger passes in a short time, but the love of God lasts forever. Further, God provides forgiveness for our sins, removing from us the reasons to be angry with us (as a kind parent would do). Why does God do this? It is because God knows we are mortals, and is understanding of our human limitations.

Living the Word

According to a little-known story, Babe Ruth, near the end of his career, was out of shape and playing poorly, getting more strike-outs than hits. It was not uncommon for him to get booed by the fans, and on this day, after striking out again, the fans booed him. However, a young child with tears in his eyes ran onto the field and threw a big hug around Babe Ruth's legs. So Babe Ruth picked up this little boy and carried him back to the sidelines, talking to him all the way. At this, the crowd stopped booing and stood, giving a silent tribute to this great ballplayer and to the boy whose love did not depend on performance.

What is God's love like? It is not like that of the crowd, who will cheer you as long as you do what they want. Surely it is much more like the love of this young boy. His love for the Babe did not depend on seeing yet another home run. Even after the disappointment of a strikeout, his love and support was there.

I wonder if we could ever "strike out" in God's eyes? After all, a professional baseball player gets only three chances to hit the ball; after two swings and misses, the batter is still allowed to step back up to the plate. But after the third miss, the batter is called "out." Suppose that after three chances we were finished too. Three chances to learn to tell the truth, or else we get called out for lying! Three chances to learn to be nice to absent people in our talk before we are called out for gossiping! Three chances to be satisfied with what we have before we are called out for greed or for coveting what belongs to our neighbors.

Actually, it seems like a good thing that God gives us more than three "swings" at learning things such as how to tell the truth, how to be nice to people even behind their back, and how to be content. And notice that I did not even mention learning to be patient, or generous, or loving to enemies!

The truth of the matter is that we often strike out when it comes to lessons like these, which are the very things that lie at the heart of the Christian walk. We may have accepted Jesus Christ as our Savior and Lord, but when we try to follow in his footsteps, we trip all over the place. Sometimes a baseball player will get fooled by a big, slow curve ball and will be so far out in front of it that the player actually gets all twisted up and falls down in the dirt by home plate. Sometimes a person who is supposed to be a follower of Christ will gossip about another person. It looks just as bad when we fall in the dirt. What kind of witness is that?

We are so lucky that the Christian life does not have a "three strikes and you are out" rule. Instead, take comfort today in the good news of the scripture. "The Lord is merciful and loving, slow to become angry and full of constant love." Notice the scripture doesn't say "love that just lasts while you are being good, or while you are hitting the ball." It says "constant love."

Let us pray:
Dear Lord, forgive me for the ways I have sinned against you and against my neighbor through my words, thoughts, and deeds. Please also forgive me for the things you wished I would have done but I left undone. Help me accept your forgiveness as another much-needed opportunity to learn and grow and improve, as I seek to become more and more like Christ, my Lord and example. Amen.

SUGGESTED PSALM: *Psalm 50*
SUGGESTED HYMNS:
   "All Hail the Power of Jesus' Name" (All)
   "Dear Lord and Father of Mankind" (B, C, E, F, L, P)

High Expectations

Hearing the Word

Both of the proverbs in the devotional reading today make an important point about the difference between righteous acts and motives. Motives are the key to true religion, not external cere-monies such as ritual sacrifices. These sayings note that if a person really wants to do God's will, it will result in actions that are fair, and an interest in doing the right thing in all of life, not just in keeping "church obligations." Note the similarity of the devo-tional scriptures to Micah 6:8 (the key verse from today's lesson scripture). That verse also stresses that God is more concerned that we do justice, love kindness, and walk humbly with God than out-wardly concern ourselves with religious rituals.

Living the Word

The movie *Short Circuit* was about a group of robots developed by the military. They were capable of performing delicate tasks such as pouring a drink, and yet they were armed with powerful laser beams that could blow up something as substantial as a tank. Still, for all their dexterity and flexibility, they were merely robots. They were obedient, but they had no particular loyalty.

Then lightning struck one of them (named "Number Five"), giv-ing life to this robot! The surge of power had given Number Five the power to think about what it had been programmed to do. Once it could think, suddenly it was less than obedient! It hitched a ride on the back of a truck heading out of the military compound, and the adventure began! The military wanted to get their secret and dangerous weapon back into their control, while the robot, now alive, wanted the freedom to do whatever it wanted to do.

Like many movies, the underlying theme of this one speaks to our life story. None of us want to be robots, manipulated by any higher power while our human capacity for choice is disregarded. An important difference between humans and robots is that humans have internal feelings and opinions, and we desire to live those out in our life. That is why religious expectations, imposed from the outside, are usually unpleasant for people who do not inwardly want a religious life. They create a conflict between what we want to do, and what some external authority is trying to force us to do.

For example, many parents must wrestle with whether to "force" a teen to go to church when the teen is not interested in God or the church. If they do so, they may wind up with a youth sitting in the pew. However, they have not really come any closer to winning that person's heart. Like a robot, the teen is only complying with external pressure; the part that is living and making choices is not yet convinced. (Please note that there are many things that are good and worth "forcing" on children, surely church is one of them for many young people. True, they have to want to go before it will become a lifelong habit, but making them go still makes a parental statement about how important it is. After all, would you let a youth decide for himself whether he liked school and therefore decide whether to pursue an education?)

The two proverbs in today's reading make the point that external compliance to religious rules, just for the sake of keeping the rules, has little value. What matters is our motivation.

You can program a robot to wash your car, bring you your slippers, and even tell you, on cue, that you look wonderful. But you cannot program a robot to like you. That is why God did not make us into creatures that would be forced to do exactly what God wanted every second. Instead, God gave us the gift of life. Ever since, we have been trying to make up our mind about where our true loyalty lies.

Our religion is meant to change our heart, our soul, our personality, our attitudes, and our true self. God doesn't want mere compliance to rules. God wants us!

Let us pray:
Dear Lord, thank you for the freedom you have given us. When we run away from you, remind us of your forgiveness, your love, and your perfect will for us. Help us turn to you inwardly, so that your spirit of love will not just change our actions, but also our heart. In Jesus' name, Amen.

100

Answering God's Call

Hearing the Word

Beginning with Paul's arrest in chapter 21, the last few chapters of Acts have to do with Paul's trial and testimony before various individuals and legal bodies, both Jewish and Roman. Today's devotional scripture comes from Paul's testimony before King Agrippa (Herod Agrippa II) and his sister Bernice, whom Paul apparently expected to be more fair and sympathetic to his case than Governor Felix had been. As evidence of this, while his fate was in Felix's hands, Paul had appealed his case to the emperor (a legal move similar to taking a case to the Supreme Court in the United States). Agrippa found him innocent of any capital offenses; but since Paul had already appealed his case to the emperor, it had to be continued in Rome. In this portion of Paul's testimony, he gives a valuable account of his conversion, explaining his motives for his actions.

Living the Word

Some people call me a "salt-water aquarium enthusiast." That means that if you stop by for a visit, you will probably get invited to see the aquarium before you go home. In fact, if the damselfish have just laid eggs, or the hermit crab has recently changed shells, I might even invite a person over just so that I can share the event!

An "enthusiast" describes someone who is greatly interested in a subject. Some people are enthusiasts about history, or race cars, or French cooking, or sports. Chances are that your friends have talked to you several times about his or her interests. Enthusiasm is catching. If you had never been interested in French cooking, but your friend is a member of the French cooking club, then there is a good chance his or her enthusiasm has resulted in you at least trying a recipe or two.

What are you an "enthusiast" for? One thing all Christians should have in common is being an enthusiast for Christ and the church. The apostle Paul talked about his faith every chance he got; in today's scripture he is even telling the king! In fact, he deliberately created chances to talk about it. If you took him a plate of cookies in prison, he would soon be telling you about Jesus. If you wrote him a letter about salt-water aquariums or the Cubs, he would write you back a letter about his faith.

If you didn't know Paul was a Christian, you didn't know Paul. It should be that way for us too. That doesn't mean we have to be pushy, but our Christian faith is one important fact about who we are. If someone really knows you, they should know you are a Christian. Even the fact that you claim the Christian faith is a witness. So claim it often! Imagine the opposite. What if everyone kept their faith a secret? Wouldn't it be a lonely feeling? Even Christians need to know they have one another, and nonbelievers will not change unless they meet a Christian enthusiast.

Try one or more of the following statements sometime, when appropriate. Chances are you won't get slapped for saying any of them. And if you do, take heart; Paul was in prison for sharing his faith, and he still kept sharing it. Some of the statements "witness" on a deeper level than others, but they all share one thing in common: They do not invade the other person's private thoughts but simply share yours, which you have the right to do.

"I just wanted you to know I prayed for you, and I'm hoping for the best!"

"I went to church Sunday and really got a lot out of the service." (Optional: "Would you like to come with me?")

"I used to be a whole different person, but when I gave my life to Christ, my life truly changed for the better."

Let us pray:
O Lord, forgive us for thinking that merely by living the faith we have witnessed enough. Since our lives still do not look perfect, help us learn to tell our story and share our beliefs in caring ways when we have the opportunity. Amen.

SUGGESTED PSALM: *Psalm 33:13-22*
SUGGESTED HYMNS:
"*Lord, I Want to Be a Christian*" (B, C, F, P, UM)
"*Praise to the Lord, the Almighty*" (B, E, F, L, P, UM, W)

Trusting God's Care

Hearing the Word

This psalm is a fairly general hymn that could have been used in any kind of worship that involved praising God. After the initial call to worship, it includes references to God's steadfast dependability, God's love, God's creative power, God's sovereignty, God's protection, and God's ability to see God's plan through in the world. Generally speaking, Jewish praise stems from God's attributes or God's character, not only from a list of things that God has done (when such a "laundry list of accomplishments" appears, it is usually to demonstrate or illustrate God's character of love or faithfulness or mercy; and it is this characteristic that deserves praise as much as the historical action).

Living the Word

On a trip to Hong Kong one spring, we had the opportunity to purchase a "name card" from a sidewalk tourist businessperson. Since the cards were small and personal, they seemed like ideal gifts to take home to our kids. You simply gave a name to the artist, and using Chinese calligraphy techniques, he painted the Chinese characters for that name on a small matted card. For example, a name like "Nicholas" consisted of three Chinese characters, written vertically on the page. I expected them to stand for the sounds "Ni," "cho," and "las." Instead, on the back of the card the characters that made up the person's name were explained. Rather than signifying sounds, each character stood for a characteristic or personality trait such as "kind," or "generous," or "brave."

Thus, "Nicholas" was named, not by a series of sounds, but by a series of characteristics. That's an intriguing concept, isn't it? Suppose that instead of using names, we were known by our characteristics! What would yours be? Some days mine would be "Here comes 'Busy, Grumpy, Tired.'" Other days it might be "Friendly, Interested, Listener." If you are really brave, ask someone what characteristics come to mind when he/she thinks of you. Or maybe you'd rather not ask! Maybe it depends on the day, as it does for most of us.

In the psalms and in Hebrew tradition, God is to be praised not only for everything God has done (or the list would make psalms like this one much longer!), but also for who God is. God's character might be described, among other things, as "Love, Mercy, Power, Creativity, Righteousness, Justice, Tender Care." It is this character, and not just the accomplishments of God, that make God praiseworthy.

It is interesting to ponder this idea while considering the name of Jesus. What scriptures come to your mind? In Matthew 1:18-25, the angel told Joseph to name the baby "Jesus" (which means "He saves"), and explained that he would also be called "Immanuel" (which means "God is with us"). Or consider Isaiah 9:6: "A child is born to us! . . . He will be called, 'Wonderful, Counselor,' 'Mighty God,' 'Eternal Father,' 'Prince of Peace' " (TEV). And think of the names Jesus used to refer to himself, such as the "light of the world," "the living water," "the way, the truth, the life," and so on.

So often in our culture we describe ourselves by what we have done and by not who we are. "I am the guy who organized the little league," or "I am the first woman to serve as mayor," or "I am a steel worker" or "I am the mother of three children." But consider all of the above, and the difference it makes whether one characteristic would be "patience." If others were to think of you in terms of your characteristics instead of your name, what would you like to have on their list?

One of the things about our relationship with the Lord is that God's good character should begin to rub off on us. That means that while our names stay the same, the description of who we are can certainly change. In fact, our Christian faith should change who we are, so that the list of characteristics that describe us begin to sound more and more like those characteristics that make our God so worthy of praise, adoration, and emulation.

Let us pray:
Dear Lord, help us become more and more like you. In Jesus' name, Amen.

SUGGESTED PSALM: *Psalm 90*

SUGGESTED HYMNS:

"*Lead On, O King Eternal*" (B, C, E, F, L, P, UM)

"*I Sing the Almighty Power of God*" (B, E, P, UM, W)

Accepting God's Judgment

Hearing the Word

Shortly after Jesus had come into Jerusalem (the "home turf" of the Jewish leaders), he came into conflict with them. This conflict is shown through their hostile questions and their attempts to trap Jesus into making statements that would alienate him from the crowd, where he had popular support. The parable Jesus tells in today's devotional scripture needs to be read against this stormy backdrop; if you read beyond the ninth verse, you will see that the Jewish leaders did not miss the jab that is buried in the story Jesus told. Further, the story implies that, first of all, Jesus is God's Son, and therefore God's last-ditch effort after sending all the prophets to get the Jewish "tenants" in God's promised land to acknowledge God and be appropriately loyal to God. Second, this story includes Jesus' ominous forecast that he, as God's Son, would be killed by the evil tenants.

Living the Word

Donald Kaul wrote a column titled "NRA Endorsement Should Be Kiss of Death" shortly after the Colorado and Georgia school shootings occurred weeks apart in the spring of 1999. In response to these shootings, there was growing public outrage about the kinds of weapons available, and in some situations without background checks required (such as at gun shows). Kaul's column pointed out that some special interest groups have such a loud voice in Washington that they can often win an issue, or at least valuable concessions, because of their monetary clout. They help elect candidates with their generous contributions, causing some legislators to vote for things that do not appear to be in the interest of the general public. One such issue, heavily influenced by special interest groups, was a bill passed by the Senate granting $7 billion in aid to Kosovo refugees. However, the amount doubled before the bill could pass, because in order to get enough senators to vote for it, some of them wanted the bill to include amendments that financed pet projects in their particular districts. It makes them look good locally when they can get money for local road improvement or other local projects.

Locally, a school board in a nearby district parted company with their superintendent before the contract was expired. Behind closed doors, an agreement was reached between the two sides to pay the superintendent $190,000 as he left. The public has demanded an explanation concerning why so much of their tax dollars was spent in that way.

Many politicians are tireless workers for the public good, and consider themselves servants of the public. They are good tenants of the public's trust. But others, once they get in power, seem to lose their responsiveness to the voters who put them in office. Instead of caring most about the public welfare, they care more about getting re-elected. It is understandable to be interested in the self, and even to be tempted to put the self above serving others. But that makes a politician a poor tenant of the office they hold. If they keep it up long enough, they will damage their good standing with the public, and the public will vote them out of office.

In the same way, we are tenants of this life God has given us. It is natural to be interested in the self and even to be tempted to put the self above serving others. But, like politicians whose political life depends on the voters, we need to be reminded whose we are and that this life of ours is rented. God is the owner and the giver. We are the servants. Let us be attentive and responsive to the Lord's will.

Let us pray:
O Lord, be with all those who hold public office, that they may serve the public good and avoid the temptation to place their personal political career above the good of the many. And in the same way, help us think of others first, that we may be more servants than selfish. In the name of Christ, Amen.

Experiencing Sin's Consequences

Hearing the Word

These verses are the beginning of the Ten Commandments, which continue on through verse 17 (and are also found in Deuteronomy 5:1-21). The reason that only some of the verses of the Ten Commandments are chosen for today's lesson is that they include the promise God makes to punish several generations of people who fail to worship God alone, but to show love to thousands of generations of those who love God and obey God's Laws. Theologically, this explains why Assyria could come and take the Israelites into captivity; only the tribe of Judah was spared this punishment sent by God through the Assyrian military.

Living the Word

According to a statistic distributed during Red Ribbon Week (October 24-31, 1998), each year almost five hundred thousand Americans die from the abuse of alcohol, tobacco, and illicit drugs. Substance abuse is the largest cause of preventable deaths in the United States. To put it in perspective, this staggering number is ten times the number of American soldiers who died in all the years of the Vietnam War put together, except that the carnage caused by substance abuse is an annual count.

Of course critics might want to contest the half-million number. Let's assume for now that even half that many people should be a source of considerable concern. Pull out your calculator. Divide 250,000 by 365 days a year, and divide that by 24 hours in a day. It comes out to more than 28 people per hour, round the clock, year in and year out, who are dying in America because of a decision someone made to abuse alcohol, tobacco, or drugs. If the actual statistic is closer to the truth, then it means that in the time it takes you to sit in an average worship service, 60 people in America die because of substance abuse while you pray and sing and worship God.

So what are you praying for this week? What does your church service mean to the teens in your church, and is your church making any attempt at all to reach the kids in your community who do not attend church?

When God gave us the Ten Commandments, God made it clear that our choices have consequences. God promised to give good consequences to those who keep God's Laws, and God said that bad consequences would come to generations of those who disregard God's Laws. Many of the consequences of sin are simply built in. If a person drinks and drives, then that decision might not only kill the person driving, but it often takes the lives of others too. And the horror that death will affect generations to come who have to grow up without a father or mother, or who must bury with their son or daughter their hope of ever having grandchildren.

So far we have spoken of substance abuse and its consequences. However, a larger point could be made. All sins have their built-in consequences. Adultery, for example, leads to the loss of trust and divorce when found out. Stealing, even when not found out, contaminates the "gain" with guilt. Lying creates the loss of integrity between who a person really is and who a person must pretend to be. And who truly feels better after a good session of ripping another person apart in gossip? Does greed lead to happiness, and lust to truly fulfilling human relationships? All sins damage us physically or mentally, and certainly spiritually. They all distance us from God, and poison our relationships with other people.

The Lord has told us what is good and right. We have gone the other way, as individuals and as a society. For that we pay a heavy price. Our hope is that God, in Christ, has paid the ultimate price to redeem us from the mess sin has put us in.

Let us pray:
Lord, have mercy upon us and upon our children and our children's children. May we follow Jesus Christ and avoid the many pitfalls of sin and its deadly consequences. Amen.